THE ABINGDON WORSHIP ANNUAL 2011

CONTEMPORARY & TRADITIONAL
RESOURCES FOR WORSHIP LEADERS

The

ABINGDON
WORSHIP
ANNUAL
2011

EDITED BY MARY J. SCIFRES & B. J. BEU

Abingdon Press
Nashville

THE ABINGDON WORSHIP ANNUAL 2011
CONTEMPORARY AND TRADITIONAL RESOURCES FOR WORSHIP LEADERS

Copyright © 2010 by Abingdon Press

All rights reserved.

This book is printed on acid-free paper.

ISBN 978-1-4267-0681-3

ISSN 1545-9322

All scripture quotations unless noted otherwise are taken from the *New Revised Standard Version of the Bible,* copyright 1989, Division of Christian Education of the National Council of the Churches of Christ in the United States of America. Used by permission. All rights reserved.

Scripture marked *Message* is taken from THE MESSAGE. Copyright © Eugene H. Peterson, 1993, 1994, 1995. Used by permission of NavPress Publishing Group.

10 11 12 13 14 15 16 17 18 19—10 9 8 7 6 5 4 3 2 1

MANUFACTURED IN THE UNITED STATES OF AMERICA

CONTENTS

May

June

July

August

September

October

CD-ROM CONTENTS

The entire print text plus the following are found only on the enclosed CD-ROM. See the ReadMe.txt file on the CD for instructions)

INTRODUCTION

A true spirit of worship is as fragile as it is beautiful and inspiring. As worship planners, you can set the mood and create an opportunity to touch the holy only to have the whole experience implode because of poorly chosen music or liturgy. Members of your congregation may love the music, enjoy the spoken and responsive liturgies, be stirred by excellent preaching, and still go away feeling somehow empty—wondering how it all tied together, wondering if they really worshiped today or if they simply enjoyed themselves, or worse yet, if they simply went through the motions. If the center does not hold, if we as worship planners throw together a hodgepodge of prayers, music, and worship experiences that have no intrinsic interconnection, how do we expect our congregations to be able to follow us as we seek to part the veil and offer a glimpse of the realm that is invisible to normal sight? If we fail in this quest through simple lack of effort, what does that say about us as worship planners? And what does it say about our commitment to the One we worship?

It takes serious planning to put together worship where everything thematically relates, where all the oars are pulling in the same direction. It is for this reason that we bring you *The Abingdon Worship Annual 2011*. In *The Abingdon Worship Annual 2011*, you will find words and ideas that focus each week's worship service alongside prayers and litanies for congregational participation. Included with this book are the full texts for each worship service on the enclosed CD-ROM. This will allow you to import printed prayers and responsive readings directly into your computer program for bulletin and program printing. The 2011 CD-ROM also includes footwashing liturgies as well as song suggestions and worship website suggestions.

When planning your services, we recommend viewing *The Abingdon Worship Annual 2011* as one invaluable piece of your worship puzzle. For additional music suggestions, we suggest consulting *Prepare! A Weekly Worship Planbook for Pastors and Musicians* or *The United Methodist Music and Worship Planner*. These resources contain lengthy listings of lectionary-related hymns, praise songs, vocal solos, and choral anthems. As you plan lectionary-based worship, preachers will find *The Abingdon Preaching Annual* an invaluable help. Worship planners and preachers can rely upon these resources to provide the words, the music, and the preaching guidance to plan integrated and coordinated worship services. Other web-based resources are listed on the enclosed CD-ROM.

The Abingdon Worship Annual 2011 contains words for worship for each Sunday of the lectionary year, along with suggestions for many of the "high" holy days. Each entry provides suggestions that follow an order of service that may be adapted to address your specific worship practice and format. Feel free to reorder or pick and choose the various resources to fit the needs of your worship services and congregations. Feel free as well to follow the suggested flow to ease your own task of planning and ordering worship.

Each entry follows a specific thematic focus arising from one or more of the week's scriptures. This focus, along with corresponding imagery, is then carried out through each of the suggested prayers and litanies for a given worship service. For those who work with contemporary worship services or who prefer more informal words, alternative ideas for those settings are offered for each service as well. Each entry includes a Call to Worship and Opening Prayer; a Prayer of Confession and Assurance of Pardon or a Unison Prayer; a Response to the Word, Offertory, or Communion Resources; and a Benediction. Additional ideas are also provided throughout this resource. We have ordered each day's suggestions to fit the Basic Pattern of Christian Worship, reflecting a flow that leads from a time of gathering and praise, into a time of receiving and responding to the word, and ending with a time of sending forth. The Praise Sentences and Contemporary Gathering Words fit the spontaneous and informal nature of many nontraditional worship styles and easily fit into the time for gathering and praise. They are often designed for use in worship without a printed program or bulletin.

Many litanies, prayers, and calls to worship in *The Abingdon Worship Annual 2011* intersperse direct quotations from scripture with lines of text from other sources. In order to focus on the poetic nature of worship words, and to facilitate the ease of use, we do not indicate these direct quotations with quotation marks.

All contributions in *The Abingdon Worship Annual 2011* are based upon readings from the *Revised Common Lectionary*. As you begin your worship planning, we encourage you to spend time with the scriptures for the day, reflecting upon them thoughtfully and prayerfully. Review the thematic ideas suggested in this resource and then read through the many words for worship provided. Listen for the words that speak to you. Let this resource be the starting point for your worship planning. As the Spirit guides you and God's word flows through you, we pray that your worship planning may be meaningful and fulfilling, for both you and your congregations. Trust God's guidance, and enjoy a wonderful year of worship and praise with your congregations!

In an attempt to provide you with a rich variety of worship experiences and perspectives, *The Abingdon Worship Annual 2011* utilizes the words of many different authors, pastors, laypersons, and theologians. Those of you who are familiar with this resource will recognize some authors from past editions, but others will be new to you. Whether new or returning, each of our authors has prayerfully studied the lections for each worship day, focused on a theme for that day, and then composed words and a suggested flow for worship to achieve a holistic, integrated worship experience. Since the contributing authors represent a wide variety of denominational and theological backgrounds, the words before you will vary in style and content. Feel free to combine or adjust the words within these pages to fit the needs of your congregation and the style of your worship services. See the copyright page for the necessary language to use when reproducing prayers and liturgies from this worship resource.

In response to requests from many of our readers, we have provided a number of communion liturgies as well. Some follow the pattern of the Great Thanksgiving; others are Prayers of Preparation and Consecration for the celebration of the Eucharist. Consult the index for a listing of these many communion resources, and feel free to use them interchangeably throughout the corresponding seasons.

On the CD-ROM, we are able to provide additional resources not found in this printed volume. For the next several years, you will find the number of electronic resources included with *The Abingdon Worship Annual* increasing and expanding. In this volume's CD-ROM, however, you will find a short list of suggested songs or hymns for each worship day, an annotated bibliography of suggested websites for worship planning, and a variety of footwashing litanies. These suggestions are offered to ease your worship planning process and increase our creativity.

We wish you God's blessings as you seek to share Christ's word and offer experiences of the Holy Spirit in your work and worship!

Mary J. Scifres and B. J. Beu, Editors

JANUARY 2, 2011

Epiphany of the Lord
Mary J. Scifres

COLOR

White

SCRIPTURE READINGS

Isaiah 60:1-6; Psalm 72:1-7, 10-14; Ephesians 3:1-12;
Matthew 2:1-12

THEME IDEAS

The Epiphany theme of light shining in the darkness contains a hidden message: the light of King Jesus is a light of
justice for the oppressed, help for the poor, and righteousness and peace to brighten a world darkened by sin
and war. News articles abound with the obvious message
that darkness still covers the earth. Yet today's scriptures
bear the good (and challenging!) news that we are heirs
to the promise in Christ Jesus and are called to bring light
in times of darkness.

INVITATION AND GATHERING

Call to Worship (Isaiah 60, Ephesians 3)
Arise, shine! Your light has come!
  The light of Christ Jesus is shining this day.
Arise, shine! *Your* light has come!
  The light of Christ Jesus is shining for us.

You are members of Christ's body
and share in Christ's promised salvation.
The light of Christ Jesus is shining in us!
Arise, shine! *You* are the light of the world.
Christ's light shines through us
with justice and peace.
Arise, shine! May our worship be filled
with light and love.

Opening Prayer (Psalm 72, Ephesians 3)

God of justice and peace,
abide in our hearts,
that we may be people of your promise.
Rain righteousness and hope
in the dry places of sin and despair.
Shower us with your glory and strength,
that we too may be instruments of your grace—
radiant beams of deliverance for the needy,
justice for the oppressed,
and caring love for the poor.
In Jesus' name, we pray. Amen.

PROCLAMATION AND RESPONSE

Prayer of Confession (Isaiah 60, Matthew 2)

Mighty God,
too often we want what is yours:
your glory and your power,
for ourselves and for our loved ones.
Humble us, we pray.
Help us remember a dirty stable
and a poor couple caring for their firstborn child,
even as King Herod used all his might
to seek the death of that holy child.
Shine in our lives with your grace and righteousness,
that we may arise as shining beacons
in a world dark with violence and oppression.

Rise up within us,
that we may grow into your likeness
and shine with the glory of love and justice.
In the name and hope of the Christ child, we pray. Amen.

Words of Assurance (Isaiah 60)

Arise, shine, dear friends! Your light has come!
The glory of God has risen upon you.
As Christ rises within us, we shine in the darkness,
for grace is ours to receive and to give.
Thanks be to God!

Passing the Peace of Christ (Ephesians 3)

As heirs to God's promise through Christ Jesus, we are all
members of the same body. Let us share in that joy as we
greet one another with signs of peace and reconciliation.

Response to the Word (Isaiah 60)

Arise, shine! Your light has come!
The light of Christ Jesus is shining in us!
Arise, shine! With Christ, you are the light
of the world.
**May Christ's light shine through us
with justice and peace.**

THANKSGIVING AND COMMUNION

Invitation to the Offering (Matthew 2)

Overwhelmed with joy, the sages of old offered their gifts
to Christ. May we share our gifts and offerings with the
same joy and humility as those wise sages did long ago.

Offering Prayer (Isaiah 60, Matthew 2)

Receive these gifts, glorious God,
as if they were those same precious gifts
of gold, frankincense, and myrrh
first offered to your child, Christ Jesus.
Shine through these gifts,
that they may become lights of hope and joy
in a world dark with despair and sorrow.

3

Shine through us,
that we may be beacons of justice and love
in all that we say and in all that we do. Amen.

The Great Thanksgiving (An Act of Preparation for Holy Communion, Epiphany)

The Lord be with you.
And also with you.
Lift up your hearts.
We lift them up to the Lord.
Let us give thanks to the Lord our God.
It is right to give our thanks and praise.

It is right, and a good and joyful thing,
always and everywhere to give thanks to you,
almighty God, creator of heaven and earth.
In ancient days, you created us in your image
to be reflections of your glory.
When we fell short, and the brilliance of your light
shining within us dimmed,
you held our hands and walked with us
out of the garden into all the corners of the earth.
From ancient times, through all the ages,
you have trusted us, redeemed us from sin,
saved us from oppression,
and proclaimed our place as your people.
In the dark wilderness of days gone by
and days yet to come, you shine as a pillar of light
and invite us to shine with you.

And so, with your people on earth,
and all the company of heaven,
we praise your name
and join their unending hymn.
**Holy, holy, holy Lord, God of power and might,
heaven and earth are full of your glory.
Hosanna in the highest. Blessed is the one
who comes in the name of the Lord.**

Hosanna in the highest.
Holy are you and blessed is the light of the world,
  Christ Jesus.
From a humble beginning to a violent death,
  Jesus shone with the light of your love and grace.
His ministry and teachings stand even today
  as beacons of justice and righteousness
  in a world too often darkened
  by oppression and sin.
Through Jesus' humble beginnings,
  you invite us to humble ourselves and live simply.
Through Christ's patient love and unfailing grace,
  you shine on us with forgiveness and deliverance,
  that as your redeemed children,
  we might shine in your world
  as signs of hope and love.

On the night when Jesus faced the darkness,
  he offered signs of light as he took the bread,
  gave thanks to you, broke the bread,
  and gave it to his disciples, saying:
  "Take, eat; this is my body which is given for you.
  Do this in remembrance of me."
When the supper was over,
  and Jesus prepared to face his darkest fears,
  he took the cup, gave thanks to you,
  and gave it, even to disciples
  who would betray and reject him, saying:
  "Drink from this, all of you; this is my life
  poured out for you and for many
  for the forgiveness of sins.
  Do this, as often as you drink it,
  in remembrance of me."

With joy and gratitude, we break this bread,
  remembering the many times Jesus was revealed
  to his disciples in the breaking of the bread.

5

In remembrance, we will take and eat this bread.
With faith and hope, we take this cup,
    remembering Jesus' ongoing gifts
    of grace and forgiveness,
    poured out for disciples
    yesterday, today, and forevermore.
In remembrance, we will take and drink of this cup.

And so, in remembrance of these your mighty acts
    and signs of light and life in Jesus Christ,
    we offer ourselves in praise and thanksgiving
    as signs of light and life
    in union with Christ's offering for us
    as we proclaim the mystery of faith.
    Christ has died.
    Christ is risen.
    Christ will come again.

Communion Prayer (Epiphany)

Pour out your Holy Spirit on all of us gathered here,
    that we may be your light in the world.
Pour out your Holy Spirit
    on these gifts of bread and wine,
    that we may be filled with your glory and grace.
By your Spirit, make us one with Christ,
    one with each other,
    and one in ministry to all the world
        until Christ comes in final victory
        and we feast at the heavenly banquet.
Through your Son, Jesus Christ,
    with the Holy Spirit in your holy church,
    all honor and glory is yours, almighty God,
        now and forever more. Amen.

Giving the Bread and Cup

*(The bread and wine are given to the people, with these or other
words of blessing.)*
The light of Christ, living in you.
The love of Christ, flowing through you.

SENDING FORTH

Benediction (Isaiah 60)
See and be radiant, for you are the light of the world.
Rejoice, for Christ has come and is shining still!
Be Christ's glory, children of God,
shining with love and hope!

CONTEMPORARY OPTIONS

Words for Reflection (Christmas, Epiphany: Isaiah 60)
In this world of darkness, Christ has come
as a beacon of hope and love.
Close your eyes and envision the darkness.
Open your eyes and see the Christ light of Christmas
shining in the candle, shining on the tree lights,
shining on the star.
Know that those lights are nothing
compared to the light living in you.
Now, look around and see Christ's light
shining in each and every one of us.
Arise, shine! Christ's light has come.
God's glory is with us now!
(This easily lends itself to a movement into the Passing of the Peace.)

Praise Sentences (Christmas, Epiphany: Isaiah 60, Matthew 2)
Christ is born!
Light has come!
Christ is born!
Light has come!
Let us come into Christ's presence
like those ancient sages, overwhelmed with joy
and prepared to worship with generosity and praise.

JANUARY 9, 2011

Baptism of the Lord
B. J. Beu

COLOR
White

SCRIPTURE READINGS
Isaiah 42:1-9; Psalm 29; Acts 10:34-43; Matthew 3:13-17

THEME IDEAS
The servant, in whom God delights, the servant, who is blessed with the power and strength of God's Spirit, focuses our readings. Isaiah proclaims that this servant will bring forth justice and righteousness. Matthew proclaims that this servant is none other than the Messiah, the fulfillment of Israel's hopes and dreams. On Baptism of the Lord Sunday, we celebrate Jesus' baptism—a baptism of both purifying water and empowering Spirit. We are a people of both water and the Spirit.

INVITATION AND GATHERING

Call to Worship (Psalm 29, Matthew 3)
The voice of God is calling over the waters:
   "Beloved, receive the Holy Spirit."
The Son of God is calling through our baptism:
   "Beloved, be born of water and the Spirit."

The Spirit of God is calling as gently
as a descending dove.
**The God of glory is thundering as wildly
as the sea.**
The voice of God is calling over the waters:
"Beloved, receive the Holy Spirit."

Opening Prayer (Isaiah 42, Psalm 29, Matthew 3)
Spirit of God,
call us once again,
that we might be a light to the nations—
a people of justice and righteousness;
a people of hope and possibility;
a people of love and care.
Descend upon us like a dove
as you alighted upon Jesus
at his baptism by John.
Wash us in the purifying waters of your baptism
and empower us with your Spirit.
Bless us this day,
that we might be born anew
in the name of our brother, Jesus Christ. Amen.

PROCLAMATION AND RESPONSE

Prayer of Confession (Acts 10, Matthew 3)
Gentle Spirit, Holy Dove,
the power of your baptism
is meant for all people,
yet we often seek it for ourselves alone;
your love is offered freely,
calling all who love you into fullness of life,
yet we act as if we alone
are your beloved children.
Forgive us when we seek to keep your gifts
for ourselves alone.
Remind us to be a light to the nations:
to open the eyes of the blind,
to free the prisoners from their chains,
to bring hope to those who sit in darkness. Amen.

9

Words of Assurance (Psalm 29, Matthew 3)

The voice that God spoke over the waters,
the voice that called to Jesus at his baptism,
speaks to us still: "You are my beloved;
receive the Holy Spirit."
As God's beloved, born of water and the Spirit,
darkness has no power over us. Amen!

Response to the Word (Isaiah 42, Psalm 29, Matthew 3)

God has blessed us with more than an understanding of
what is good and pleasing. God has blessed us with new
life and power through the gift of the Holy Spirit. Heed
the voice that calls to you over the waters. Rejoice in the
glory of God that thunders for all the world to hear. Sing
praise to the one who was baptized by John, that we
might become his disciples and children of the living God.

THANKSGIVING AND COMMUNION

Offering Prayer (Psalm 29, Acts 8)

Gracious God,
for the joy of our baptism,
we thank you;
for new life in your Spirit,
we praise you;
for the opportunity to become Christ's disciples,
we offer you our heartfelt gratitude.
Receive these gifts,
that they may be symbols of our commitment
to honor our baptism
in all that we do and in all that we say. Amen.

Invitation to Reaffirm Our Baptismal Covenant

The voice of God is calling:
"Come to the healing waters and be made whole."
Make us whole, O God.
The voice of Christ is calling:

"Receive the fire of the Spirit and be reborn."
Give us life anew, Great Spirit.
The voice of God is calling:
"Come."

SENDING FORTH

Benediction (Psalm 29, Matthew 3)
The son of God calls to us through our baptism:
"Beloved, receive the Holy Spirit."
The Spirit of God descends upon us like a dove.
We are born of water and the Spirit.
The voice of God sends us forth,
renewed and made whole.
**Blessed by water and the Spirit,
we go forth as a blessing to all.**

CONTEMPORARY OPTIONS

Gathering Words (Isaiah 42)
Come to the river of life.
We are a people of the water.
Splash and play in holy springs.
We are a people of the water.
Be baptized and receive the Holy Spirit.
We are a people of the water.
Come to the river of life.

Praise Sentences (Psalm 29)
Praise the God of glory and strength!
Worship the Lord in holy splendor!
Praise the Son who sits enthroned as King forever.
Worship the Lord in holy splendor!
Praise the Spirit who gives us life.
Worship the Lord in holy splendor!

JANUARY 16, 2011

Second Sunday after the Epiphany
Laura Jaquith Bartlett

COLOR
Green

SCRIPTURE READINGS
Isaiah 49:1-7; Psalm 40:1-11; 1 Corinthians 1:1-9;
John 1:29-42

THEME IDEAS
It's hard to ignore a scripture passage that begins, "Listen
to me...pay attention, you peoples!" (Isaiah 49:1). God is
definitely trying to get our attention! It is clear from this
text (and from the world around us) that there is plenty of
work to be done in the task of building up God's realm. In
fact, a quick glance at the newspapers and TV reports could
easily cause us to be overwhelmed by the magnitude of the
task. Yet both the Isaiah and 1 Corinthians readings assure
us that we are not only called to do God's work, we are well
equipped by the very One who has called us. Our faithful
God strengthens us for the task and has already given us
the support we need through Jesus Christ.

INVITATION AND GATHERING

Call to Worship (Isaiah 49, The Message)
Listen up, everyone!
God has given us work to do.
God has called each of us
before we were even born.
It was God who named us.
It is God who claims us.
The light of God's love shines in us.
Let's shine God's love into all the world!

Opening Prayer (Isaiah 49, 1 Corinthians 1)
God of Isaiah,
    you are our God, too.
You spoke to the prophets,
    but your message did not end with them.
There is still work to be done,
    and we pray to hear your call afresh.
Help us joyfully claim our role
    as your beloved servants,
        knowing that you provide all that we need
            to do our work.
You walked with us before we were even born,
    and you continue to hold us by the hand
        each and every day of our lives.
We pray with the confidence of those
    who have been filled with your light.
We pray with the assurance of those
    who have been called into fellowship
        with your Son, Jesus Christ. Amen.

PROCLAMATION AND RESPONSE

*Prayer of Confession (Isaiah 49, Psalm 40,
1 Corinthians 1)*
Faithful God,
    you call us to be saints,
        but we are more comfortable

with the role of sinner;
you call us to be your servants,
but we worry that we lack the skills
to do your work;
you put a new song of praise in our mouths,
but we stumble on unfamiliar words;
you show us the work to be tackled,
but we turn away defiant,
insisting we have more important things to do.
Put your song on our lips and in our hearts,
and remind us of the joy that awaits us
when we put our trust in you.
Guide us into the light
of your unwavering, never-ending,
and grace-filled love. Amen.

Words of Assurance (1 Corinthians 1)
God is faithful and ever-present.
The God who knew us before our birth
loves us still and strengthens us,
that we will one day be blameless.
Through the gift of Jesus Christ,
God offers forgiveness, grace, and mercy.
Enter into the light!

Response to the Word (Isaiah 49, Psalm 40)
*(Sing stanza 1 of "I Was There to Hear Your Borning Cry" by
John Ylvisaker. Continue the instrumental music quietly in the
background during the spoken responses.)*
Even before you were born, I have been with you.
My love for you is beyond time.
Fill us with your love.
Equip us for your work.
(Sing stanzas 2 and 3)
I have given you a song of praise.
I will teach you a new melody.
Fill us with your music.
Equip us to sing your harmonies.

(Sing stanzas 4 and 5)
You are my faithful servants.
I offer you all that you need
to do the work given you.
   Fill us with your Spirit.
   Equip us to share your love with the world.
(Sing stanzas 6 and 7)
Even before you were born, I have been with you.
My love for you is beyond time.
   Fill us with your light.
   Equip us to become beacons of your salvation.

THANKSGIVING AND COMMUNION

Offering Prayer (Isaiah 49, Psalm 40, 1 Corinthians 1)

Generous God,
   you have already given us all that we need.
Help us trust your continued care,
   that we may share with others
      the abundance of your blessings.
Strengthen us for service,
   and remind us of the great joy
      that awaits those who answer your call.
Accept our gifts and give us new songs of praise
   as we celebrate the opportunity to be in ministry,
      in the name of your Son, Jesus Christ. Amen.

SENDING FORTH

Benediction (Isaiah 49, 1 Corinthians 1)

Go in the love of the One who strengthens us
   for the work to which we are called.
Go in the fellowship of Jesus Christ,
   who claims us as sisters and brothers.
Go in the community of the Holy Spirit,
   who binds us together with all the saints.

Go with grace to shine God's love
into all the world. Amen.

CONTEMPORARY OPTIONS

Gathering Words (Isaiah 49, Psalm 40)

*(This dialogue for two voices should be rehearsed ahead of time,
with no text printed in the bulletin. Be ready to move directly into
an opening song: e.g., "We Are Called" or "Shine, Jesus, Shine.")*

Voice 1: Hey, everybody! God has a job for us!

Voice 2: Who does?

Voice 1: God! The God who has known you, even before you were born.

**Voice 2: What are you talking about?
How could someone know me before there
was anyone to know?**

Voice 1: I'm talking about God! God has known all
about you since forever.

Voice 2: Ummm... sounds kind of creepy.

Voice 1: It's not creepy, it's fabulous!
This is a God who has always known and
loved you, and will always love you no matter what.

Voice 2: That's amazing! So what's the job?

Voice 1: Spread the news! Share the love! Shine the
light! Sing the song!

**Voice 2: Hey, slow down! That's a big job. Can't God
just take care of it?**

Voice 1: God *is* taking care of it—by giving you what
you need to do the job. God has chosen *you*!

**Voice 2: Well, it's hard to argue with someone who
has known me since before I was born. So
what's that song you mentioned?**

Voice 1: Let's start singing right now!

Praise Sentences (Isaiah 49, Psalm 40, 1 Corinthians 1)

God is faithful.
God's steadfast love and faithfulness

keep us safe forever.
God is faithful.
The Holy One of Israel has chosen you.
God is faithful.
**By God, you were called into fellowship
with our Lord, Jesus Christ.**
God is faithful.
Let us worship God!

JANUARY 23, 2011

Third Sunday after the Epiphany

Mary Petrina Boyd

COLOR

Green

SCRIPTURE READINGS

Isaiah 9:1-4; Psalm 27:1, 4-9; 1 Corinthians 1:10-18;
Matthew 4:12-23

THEME IDEAS

In the darkness of winter, these scriptures shine forth with
the light of grace. Isaiah speaks of light coming to those in
the deep darkness of anguish; Psalm 27 calls the Lord "my
light"; and Jesus fulfills the promise of Isaiah as he begins
his ministry. The light of God calls people to rejoice and to
follow Jesus into a ministry of teaching, preaching, and
healing. The light of God calls us to remember our essential unity and our need for one another. By the light of
love, we find that the foolishness of the world is the power
of God.

INVITATION AND GATHERING

Call to Worship (Isaiah 9)

We walk in darkness.
We live in a land of deep darkness.

18

We have seen a great light!
Light shines upon us!
God brings us joy!
Rejoice before our God!

—*Or*—

Call to Worship (Psalm 27)

The Lord is our light and our salvation!
Why should we be afraid?
The Lord is the stronghold of our life!
What have we to fear?
Let us shout with joy to God!
Let us sing and make music before our God.

Opening Prayer (Psalm 27)

O God, our light and our salvation,
shelter us in your love.
O God, our stronghold,
protect us from danger.
We come with shouts of joy
to worship you this day.
We come with song and music
to celebrate your love.
We come with longing
to seek your presence.
Be with us now, O God,
as we sing your praises. Amen.

PROCLAMATION AND RESPONSE

Prayer of Confession (Isaiah 9, Psalm 27, 1 Corinthians, Matthew 9)

God of light,
we live in the darkness of despair:
worried about our lives,
concerned for our health,
fearful that we are lost from you.

The yoke of our burdens lies heavy upon us:
 our unwillingness to forgive,
 our fears of one another,
 our reluctance to share what we have,
 our divisions and quarrels.
We long to turn from the dark
 and live in the light.
We yearn to leave what is evil
 and follow the paths of righteousness.
Shine the light of your love upon us
 and transform us with your love,
  that your promised realm may draw near. Amen.

Words of Assurance (Psalm 27)

The light of God's love
 shines into the dark places of our world,
  healing its brokenness,
   and bringing hope to places of despair.
The light of God's love
 makes us a forgiven people.
Thanks be to God!

Passing the Peace of Christ (Matthew 4)

The light of Christ shines brightly in the darkened places
of our lives, bringing healing and hope. The light of Christ
shines brightly in the faces of our neighbors. Look for that
light as we share Christ's peace.

Response to the Word (1 Corinthians 1, Matthew 4)

God of love,
 we hear your call to follow.
May we see that the foolishness of your word
 is more powerful than the wisdom of this world.
May we lay aside our differences
 for the sake of the gospel.
Your realm of light and life has drawn near;
 we hear your word of truth.

Turn our hearts toward you
 and give us the wisdom to walk in your ways. Amen.

THANKSGIVING AND COMMUNION

Invitation to the Offering (Matthew 4)

Beside the lakeshore, long ago, Jesus called to his disciples: "Follow me, and I will make you fish for people!" Jesus calls to us today: "Follow me, and I will make you fish for people." The ministry begun by the Sea of Galilee continues in our day when we proclaim the good news of God's love. Let us give with joy as we follow Jesus.

Offering Prayer (Isaiah 9, Matthew 4)

O God,
 we have seen your glory,
 felt the touch of your love,
  and felt your presence with us.
With joyful hearts,
 we offer you our gifts.
Having heard your call,
 we offer you our lives and our service. Amen.

Great Thanksgiving (Isaiah 9, Matthew 4)

Almighty God, we rejoice in the light of your love
 as we praise you at all times and in all places.
In the beginning, as you created the world,
 you said, "Let there be light."
You looked and saw that the light was good.
You made the sun, moon, and stars,
 that they might mark the seasons of the earth.
You created us in your image,
 that we might live in the light
 and care for your world.
When anguish and despair darkened the earth,
 you sent your prophets to call the people
 to faithfulness and to proclaim your promises.
To those in darkness, you sent a great light,
 that they might see your ways
 and rejoice before you.

And so, with your people on earth,
and all the company of heaven,
we praise your name
and join their unending hymn.
Holy, holy, holy Lord, God of power and might,
Heaven and earth are full of your glory.
Hosanna in the highest. Blessed is the one
who comes in the name of the Lord.
Hosanna in the highest.

In the fullness of time, you sent your Son, Jesus Christ,
the light of the world, to claim us as your own.
He taught your ways, proclaimed the good news,
and healed the sick.
In him we see the light of your love.
Through him, you have gathered us
into the body of Christ and made us one,
that we too might reflect your light to the world.

(Words of Institution)

SENDING FORTH

Benediction (Matthew 4)
Jesus, the light of the world, calls us to follow.
Go and tell the news of God's love.
Cast the nets of grace wide,
that all may see the glory of God.
Go forth and shine with God's light!
May God—Source, Word, and Spirit—
bless you with the radiance of love.

CONTEMPORARY OPTIONS

Gathering Words (Matthew 4)
Jesus calls, "Follow me!"
We will follow Jesus.

Jesus calls, "Follow me!"
We will leave the past to follow Jesus.
Jesus calls, "Follow me!"
We will walk in the present to follow Jesus.
Jesus calls, "Follow me!"
We will follow Jesus.

Praise Sentences (Isaiah 9, Matthew 4)

Jesus is the light of the world!
The light shines in the darkness.
We rejoice with joy!

JANUARY 30, 2011

Fourth Sunday after the Epiphany
Joanne Carlson Brown

COLOR
Green

SCRIPTURE READINGS
Micah 6:1-8; Psalm 15; 1 Corinthians 1:18-31;
Matthew 5:1-12

THEME IDEAS
Who are the people of God? Not those with correct beliefs
or worldly wisdom, but those who act with justice and
compassion, who walk humbly with their God; those
whom the world might call foolish because they choose
to live kingdom values rather than worldly values; those
who go against the status quo and work to bring about
God's beloved community on earth, here and now.

INVITATION AND GATHERING

*Call to Worship (Micah 6, Psalm 15, Matthew 5,
1 Corinthians 1)*
People of God, who do you come to worship?
We come to worship the one true God.
How will you worship?
**Not with words alone, but by living lives
of justice and love.**

Come, you who belong to God.
Come, you who are foolish in the eyes of the world.
Come and abide in God's tent and in God's heart,
now and forever.

Unison Opening Prayer (Micah 6, Psalm 15, Matthew 5, 1 Corinthians 1)

Loving God,
  we come this morning
    seeking to abide in your presence.
Open our minds to your spirit of wisdom,
  that we may know how to live as your people.
Open our hearts to your spirit of truth,
  that we may love all your people with a love
    that speaks of justice, kindness,
      and radical grace.
May this time of worship
  be authentic and pleasing to you. Amen.

PROCLAMATION AND RESPONSE

Prayer of Confession (Micah 6, Psalm 15, Matthew 5, 1 Corinthians 1)

Far too often, O God,
  we desire to look wise
    in the eyes of the world.
We have not spoken truth with our hearts.
We have said and done hurtful things to our friends.
We have forgotten our true identity,
  wandering into ways that are not yours.
We have lost the path of true worship,
  focusing on form and words rather than deeds.
We have forgotten what true discipleship is.
And because of this, you have a quarrel with us.
Forgive us and help us live into becoming
  the people you have created and called us to be:
    people of justice and love and truth
      and humility, and yes, even foolishness.

May we be fools for Christ,
    embracing our true identity,
    even in the face of the world's scorn and derision.

Words of Assurance (Micah 6, Matthew 5)

God has called us and blesses us
    when we live God's ways and not the world's.
God's love embraces us
    even when we fall short of what God desires
    for our lives and actions.
Know that the God of blessing
    loves and forgives us with a fierce tenderness.
And in so knowing, may our lives and souls
    be transformed.

Passing the Peace of Christ (Matthew 5)

The God of blessing and love be with all of us.
    We embrace God's blessing and love.
Turn now and pass that blessing on to one another
so that our community may be bound together
in love and blessing.

Response to the Word (Micah 6, Matthew 5, 1 Corinthians 1)

For the words of challenge,
for the words of blessing,
for the spirit of wisdom moving in our midst,
    we give you honor and thanks and praise.

THANKSGIVING AND COMMUNION

Invitation to the Offering (Micah 6, Matthew 5)

We have been called to lives of justice, love, and truth. We have been blessed to be a blessing. Let us generously offer all that we are and all that we have to further this beloved community of love, justice, truth, and blessing.

Offering Prayer (Micah 6, Matthew 5)

O God,
    you bless us in so many areas of our lives—
        in places we often fail to recognize as blessing.

Help us have eyes to see and hearts to understand
   the depth of your love and blessing.
Today, we give out of that blessedness,
   dedicating ourselves to lives of justice and love,
   giving all that we are and all that we have
     to bring about your beloved community,
      here and now. Amen.

SENDING FORTH

Benediction (Micah 6, Psalm 15, Matthew 5)

Those who live lives pleasing to God
   shall not be moved.
Go now to embrace the kingdom values—
   values of love, justice, and truth.
Go now with God's blessing,
   to live those values through the power
   of our challenging, faithful, loving,
   empowering God. Amen.

CONTEMPORARY OPTIONS

Gathering Words (Micah 6, Matthew 5, 1 Corinthians 1)

Come and hear the good news.
No matter what is happening in your life,
   God's blessing and love is with you.
Come and hear what God wants you to do:
   live lives of justice and love and truth.
Come and get courage and strength
   to be fools for Christ,
   embracing Kingdom values
   rather than those of the world.
We're here, ready to listen, open to change,
   expecting to be blessed by our time together.

Praise Sentences (Micah 6, Psalm 15, Matthew 5, 1 Corinthians 1)
Our God is a God of blessing.
Our God is a God of love and justice.
Our God is a God of wisdom and truth.
Living and loving in that spirit,
    we will not be moved.

FEBRUARY 6, 2011

Fifth Sunday after the Epiphany
Mary J. Scifres

COLOR
Green

SCRIPTURE READINGS
Isaiah 58:1-9a, (9b-12); Psalm 112:1-9, (10);
1 Corinthians 2:1-12, (13-16); Matthew 5:13-20

THEME IDEAS
Today's readings from Isaiah and Matthew illuminate the
Epiphany theme of light shining in the darkness. We are
called to be salt and light, to flavor and shine upon the
earth with justice and righteousness. Isaiah vividly illustrates Jesus' warning that our righteousness must be more
than just words and worship. Rather, we are called to live
our worship, by acting as God's love and compassion for
the world.

INVITATION AND GATHERING

Call to Worship (Isaiah 58, Matthew 5)
Shout out! You are the light of the world!
We lift up our voices and sing praises to God!
Live your praise with justice and love.
**We lift up our lives with compassion
and mercy.**
Let us enter God's house as bearers of light.

Opening Prayer (Isaiah 58, Psalm 112, Matthew 5)
> God of justice and mercy, Christ of light and life,
>> enter our lives and this time of worship
>>> with your radiant presence.
>
> Bring light to our journey,
>> that we may see your path of righteousness.
>
> Shine in us and through us,
>> that we may be lights of compassion and justice
>>> for all the world to see. Amen.

PROCLAMATION AND RESPONSE

Prayer of Confession (Isaiah 58, Matthew 5)
> Compassionate One,
>> forgive us when our compassion runs short;
>> forgive us when we worship in word
>>> but not in truth;
>> forgive us when we side with the powerful
>>> rather than the poor and meek.
>
> Shine into the dark places of our lives
>> and into the shadowy depths of our souls.
>
> In your grace and mercy,
>> transform us into vessels of light,
>> that we might be lamps shining on a hill
>>> with compassion and kindness,
>>>> justice and mercy.
>
> Loosen the bonds of sin and selfishness within us,
>> that we might loosen the bonds
>>> of injustice and oppression in our world.
>
> In Christ's name, we pray. Amen.

Words of Assurance (Isaiah 58, Matthew 5)
> When we accept Christ's gift of grace,
>> God releases us from the yoke of sin and sorrow,
>> and we are able to live as God's chosen ones.
>
> When we loosen the bonds of injustice
>> and the yoke of oppression,
>> we are living vessels of light.

Rejoice, sisters and brothers,
  our light shall rise in the darkness,
  and we shall shine for all to see!

Passing the Peace of Christ (Matthew 5)
You are the light of the world! Let your light shine before others as we turn to one another to offer signs of light and peace.

Response to the Word (Isaiah 58, Psalm 112, Matthew 5)
When we free ourselves from the bonds of injustice,
  we are the light of the world!
When we undo the yoke of oppression,
  we are the light of the world!
When we share our bread with the hungry,
  we are the light of the world!
When we bring shelter to the homeless,
  we are the light of the world!
When we clothe the naked and give to the poor,
  we are the light of the world!
Let us be light and salt, children of righteousness,
Christ Jesus for all the world.
  Amen!

THANKSGIVING AND COMMUNION

Invitation to the Offering (Psalm 112)
Happy are those who love the Lord! It is well with those who share generously and conduct their lives with justice and mercy. Let us share this joy as we give of ourselves as we collect this morning's offering.

Offering Prayer (Isaiah 58, Matthew 5)
God of light and love,
  shine through these offerings,
  that our love may radiate
    throughout the world.

Make bright the hope of justice and mercy
in places of darkness and fear.
Guide our paths,
that we may always be
lights of compassion and care
for a world in need.

The Great Thanksgiving (An Act of Preparation for Holy Communion)
(Use the Great Thanksgiving for January 2, 2011, p. 00)

SENDING FORTH

Benediction (Isaiah 58, Matthew 5)
Shout out! Do not hold back!
I am the light of the world!
Lift up your voice with joy and praise.
I am the light of the world!

—Or—

Benediction (Isaiah 58, Matthew 5)
You are the light of the world!
You are the salt of the earth!
Go forth with compassion, mercy, and grace.
Go forth with confidence, strength, and hope,
shining for all to see!

CONTEMPORARY OPTIONS

Gathering Words (Matthew 5)
Light and salt, we are called to be.
We are the light of the world?
Light and salt, we are created to become.
We are the salt of the earth?
Light and salt, we are Christ for the world.
We are the light and salt of the world!

Praise Sentences (Matthew 5)
You are the light of the world!
Rejoice with shouts of praise!

You are the salt of the earth!
Rejoice with shouts of praise!
Christ is in us, shining with love.
Rejoice with shouts of praise!

FEBRUARY 13, 2011

Sixth Sunday after the Epiphany
Mary Petrina Boyd

COLOR

Green

SCRIPTURE READINGS

Deuteronomy 30:15-20; Psalm 119:1-8;
1 Corinthians 3:1-9; Matthew 5:21-37

THEME IDEAS

God calls us to walk in ways that lead to life and abundance. In his final address, Moses urges the Hebrew people to choose life; the psalmist praises those who walk in
God's ways; and Jesus calls for a deeper, more faithful understanding of God's laws. Jesus calls us to reconcile with
one another, to love faithfully, and to speak truthfully. Lest
this lead us to think that salvation comes only through
human endeavors, Paul reminds us that God alone gives
the growth.

INVITATION AND GATHERING

Call to Worship (Psalm 119)

Happy are those who are without blame.
Blessed are those who walk in God's way.
Happy are those who are faithful.
Blessed are those who seek God.

We will obey your word, O God.
We will praise you forever!

Opening Prayer (Deuteronomy 30, Psalm 119)

Come, Holy One:
    teach us your ways,
    lead us in your paths,
    guide us on our journey.
Speak to us your words of life,
    for you offer us direction and wholeness
        when we hear your voice
            and follow.
You bless us with your love,
    shower us with your grace,
        and help us grow in faith.
We seek you, O God,
    with all our hearts.
Be near us this day. Amen.

PROCLAMATION AND RESPONSE

Prayer of Confession (Deuteronomy 30, 1 Corinthians 3, Mark 5)

Loving God,
    you call us into community,
    teach us your ways,
        and bless us with abundant life.
Yet we turn aside to follow other paths:
    we take the easy way out,
        listening to the world's call
            rather than your call to commitment;
    we quarrel with one another,
        letting differences divide us;
    we cherish our resentments,
        shutting off our hearts
            from forgiveness and reconciliation;
    we cling to petty jealousies,
        feeling we deserve more than we have.

Forgive us when we wander from your love.
Draw us into community with each other,
   and feed us with the milk of your grace,
   that we may grow in faithfulness
     and work together in peace. Amen.

Words of Assurance (Deuteronomy 30, 1 Corinthians 3)
God is at work, nurturing our growth
   and showing us the ways that lead to life.
God is at work, reconciling us to one another
   and teaching us the paths of love.
God is at work, hearing our confessions,
   forgiving our disobedience,
   and blessing us in love.
Thanks be to God!

Passing the Peace of Christ (Matthew 5)
Christ asks that we be reconciled to one another. The love
of Christ reaches out to friend and stranger, touching each
life with blessing. Share the peace and forgiveness of
Christ with one another.

Response to the Word (Deuteronomy 30, Matthew 5)
Caring God,
   nurture the life within us.
You have shown us the ways
   that lead to life.
You have challenged us
   to move beyond easy answers,
   to embrace the hard choices
     that come with caring deeply for others.
Give us the wisdom and the courage
   to resist evil and walk in your ways of love. Amen.

THANKSGIVING AND COMMUNION

Invitation to the Offering (Deuteronomy 30, 1 Corinthians 3)
God has given us growth, guided our steps on the ways
that lead to life, and provided companions for our jour-

ney. Our very lives are a gift from God. With gratitude and praise, we turn to God with obedient hearts to offer back our gifts, that others may find life and wholeness.

Offering Prayer (Deuteronomy 30, Matthew 5)
Loving God,
>you have shown us your ways
>>and led us in the paths of abundance.

You have blessed us and kept us safe.
In you we see that we are loved.
We offer you our lives,
>for we have chosen to follow you.

We offer you our praise,
>for your love is great.

Use our gifts, our money, and our hearts
>to establish your realm of love upon the earth. Amen.

Invitation to Communion (Matthew 5, 1 Corinthians 3)
This is Christ's table, where all are welcome. Here we are fed in abundance. Here we gather as Christ's body. Reconciled to one another, we are God's people. We are God's servants, working together. We are God's field, where love is sown. We are God's building, a house of love. The feast is prepared; the table is ready. Come! Rejoice and be fed.

SENDING FORTH

Benediction (Deuteronomy 30)
Go forth to walk in God's ways.
>**May our ways be blameless.**

Hold fast to God in all you do.
>**Our hearts belong to God.**

May the love of God be yours.
>**God's blessings rest upon us.**

CONTEMPORARY OPTIONS

Gathering Words (Deuteronomy 30)
Choose life!
>**We will love the Lord our God.**

Choose life!
We will obey God in all we do.
Choose life!
We will hold fast to our God.
Choose life!
We choose life in God's love!

Praise Sentences (Deuteronomy 30)

Choose life! Choose God!
Live in God's love!
God's way is good!
Hold fast to God!

FEBRUARY 20, 2011

Seventh Sunday after the Epiphany
Jamie D. Greening

COLOR
Green

SCRIPTURE READINGS
Leviticus 19:1-2, 9-18; Psalm 119:33-40;
1 Corinthians 3:10-11, 16-23; Matthew 5:38-48

THEME IDEAS
The first two verses of Leviticus 19 convey the overall emphasis of today's readings: God is holy and God's people must be holy. Through prayer, the psalmist depicts holiness as a hunger to know and walk in God's ways. The epistle reminds us that we belong to God as a holy building, as a temple. The key to this holiness is to be foolish to the world but wise to God. Finally, the parallels between the Gospel reading and our Leviticus text remind us that Jesus' Sermon on the Mount was a commentary on Old Testament Law. Moses and Jesus both remind us that holiness is as much about ethics as it is about worship.

INVITATION AND GATHERING

Call to Worship (Leviticus 19, Psalm 119, 1 Corinthians 3)

Hear the word of God:
"You shall be holy, for I am holy."
We choose holiness and reject futile thinking.
We look today at life and turn our eyes
from the vanities of this world.
We want to be holy, for the Lord is holy.
We affirm that we belong to Christ.
We crave his wisdom and his ways.
(This reading could be followed by the hymn "Holy, Holy, Holy"
or the praise song "Holiness.")

Opening Prayer (Psalm 119, Matthew 5)

Almighty Teacher,
  instruct us in your statutes today.
Help us turn the other cheek when we are wronged
  and do so without bitterness.
Inspire us to give to those in need
  and do so without resentment.
Turn our hearts,
  that we may learn how to love our neighbor,
    even our enemies.
Teach us and show us the way of holiness,
  that we may be a holy people. Amen.

PROCLAMATION AND RESPONSE

Prayer of Confession (Leviticus 19, Matthew 5)

(Station Reader 1 at the front of the worship space and Reader
2 at the rear, thereby putting the people in the midst of the
prayer.)

Reader 1: Holy God, forgive us for our sins against our
           community.
Reader 2: We have not provided for the poor or the
           alien in our land. We have not paid just
           wages to those who labor. We have made life

difficult for the blind, deaf, and those with special needs. We have rendered improper judgments about right and wrong. We have done harm to the environment.

Reader 1: Holy Jesus, forgive our sins against our neighbors.

Reader 2: We have not been generous. We have not prayed for our neighbors' needs. We have slandered friends and foes alike. We have loved ourselves more than we love others.

People: Holy Spirit, thank you for the assurance of forgiveness. Help us move beyond our sin, that we may make the world a better place to live. Amen.

Words of Assurance (1 Corinthians 3)

We belong to Christ:
   our past belongs to Christ;
   our sins belong to Christ.
We belong to Christ:
   our right now belongs to Christ;
   our moment of forgiveness belongs to Christ.
We belong to Christ:
   our future belongs to Christ;
   our holy future, free of guilt and shame,
      belongs to Christ.

Passing the Peace of Christ (Matthew 5)

That we may all be as daughters and sons of God, our Mother and our Father, let us greet one another with signs of peace and blessing, affirming that God desires love and kindness to all.

Response to the Word (Psalm 119)

By your word, O Lord,
   you have taught us.
May your Holy Spirit
   grant us understanding and guidance
      to live your word.
Lead us in the right paths

of true spirituality.
Turn our hearts and our eyes toward Jesus
    and confirm in our souls
        the beauty of your ways. Amen.

THANKSGIVING AND COMMUNION

Invitation to the Offering (Leviticus 19, 1 Corinthians 3)

If we learn nothing else from Leviticus, we learn that the Lord cares how we use our financial resources. God cares whether we help the poor, pay just wages, or steal from others. The so-called wisdom of our time is oppressive and power hungry, devaluing benevolence, charity, creation care, and equality. But Christ, in whom we believe, values these things, and so must we. We belong to God, and all we have belongs to the Lord. Let us show what we believe by being holy with our money.

Offering Prayer (Leviticus 19, Matthew 5)

We bring these offerings to you, O Lord,
    not because you need them,
        but because you are holy.
Through these resources
    we ask that he who is without a cloak be clothed,
        and she who is hungry be fed.
We bring these offerings before you
    and ask that they be used
        to fulfill your holy purposes. Amen.

SENDING FORTH

Benediction (Leviticus 19, 1 Corinthians 3)

If you belong to Christ, then you belong to God.
    We belong to Christ; we are God's.
Go and be holy in the world, as God is holy.
    We will walk in the way of holiness,
    giving glory to God in all we do.

CONTEMPORARY OPTIONS

Gathering Words (Psalm 119, 1 Corinthians 3)

Have you had enough of the wisdom of the world?
Yes, we've had enough!
Do you want to know true wisdom?
Yes, we do!
Do you want to be taught, given, led, and confirmed
in the holiness of Christ Jesus, our Lord?
Yes, we long for this.
Come and embrace the ways of God,
the ways of true life and wisdom.

Praise Sentences (Leviticus 19)

Speak to the congregation.
God is holy.
Speak to the community.
God is holy.
Speak to the whole world.
God is holy.
God is holy.
God is holy.

FEBRUARY 27, 2011

Eighth Sunday after the Epiphany
Mary J. Scifres

COLOR
Green

SCRIPTURE READINGS
Isaiah 49:8-16a; Psalm 131; 1 Corinthians 4:1-5;
Matthew 6:24-34

THEME IDEAS
Overcoming worry through trust is the challenge and gift
that Jesus offers in today's reading from Matthew. Even
in Isaiah's prophecy and David's gentle psalm, we are
called to trust in the midst of exile and suffering and to
hope in the midst of doubt and despair. As we learn
to trust, we find bread for the journey and comfort for
the soul.

INVITATION AND GATHERING

Call to Worship (Isaiah 49, Matthew 6)
Do not worry about your life,
for we are held in the palm of God's hand.
We gather this day as people of hope,
striving to trust in God's care.
Do not fret about the clothes you will wear,
for we are clothed in the loving compassion of Christ.

We gather this day as people of hope,
striving to trust in God's grace.
Do not think about what you will eat,
for we are filled with the Spirit of God.
We gather this day as people of hope,
striving for the kingdom of God.

Opening Prayer (Isaiah 49, Psalm 131, 1 Corinthians 4, Matthew 6)

God of constant care and compassion,
grace us this day with your presence.
Help us lay aside our burdens and trust in your love,
that we may be led by your guiding hand
and clarifying light.
Aid us as we seek your heavenly hopes for this earth,
that we may be children of your womb
and reflections of your light and life. Amen.

PROCLAMATION AND RESPONSE

Responsive Prayer of Confession and Words of Assurance (Isaiah 49, Matthew 6)

Sing for joy with heaven and earth!
But we are haunted by worry and doubt.
Break forth into song with the mountains and hills!
But we are caught in valleys of darkness.
Trust in our God, who cares for us all.
But we are burdened by loads too heavy to bear.
God cares for our burdens and lifts up our hearts.
But we are weary and lonely for help.
Trust in Christ Jesus, who has borne all our grief
and has written our names in the palm of God's hand.
We are forgiven, cared for, and loved.
We are forgiven, cared for, and loved?
We are forgiven, cared for, and loved.
Sing for joy with heaven and earth!
We are forgiven, cared for, and loved!

Passing the Peace of Christ (Isaiah 49, Matthew 6)
As God forgives, cares for, and loves us, let us share signs of forgiveness, caring, and love with one another.

Response to the Word (Matthew 6)
Reflecting upon today's scriptures and messages of hope, let us examine the worries that haunt our lives; let us release our burdens to God and be free.

(Invite people to a time of silence or small-group conversation to name concerns, stresses, or worries that prevent them from trusting God's providential love. You may ritualize this with concerns written on paper to be burned, nailed to a cross, or placed as an offering for God to carry. You may also ritualize this in the form of verbal prayer with and for one another.)

Do not worry, but hope in our God, whose caring compassion is enough.

THANKSGIVING AND COMMUNION

Invitation to the Offering (Matthew 6)
When we try to serve both God and money, we only create burdens of worry and stress. Let us release ourselves from our bondage by sharing and giving generously, remembering that all we have and all we are is a gift and a trust from God.

Offering Prayer (Isaiah 49, 1 Corinthians 4, Matthew 6)
Compassionate God,
    imbue these gifts
        with your grace and your care.
Inscribe your very name
    on the ministries and the people
        that these gifts will support.
Let them become signs of hope for those in despair,
    a light for the journey when darkness descends. Amen.

SENDING FORTH

Benediction (Isaiah 49, Matthew 6)

Do not worry about your life,
what you will eat or drink or wear.
We will hope in our God,
and trust in Christ's gracious love.
Go forth with songs of joy!

CONTEMPORARY OPTIONS

Gathering Words (Isaiah 49)

O sing for joy, children of earth!
The heavens are singing today!
Break forth into singing, climbers of mountains!
The heavens are singing today!
Walk confidently in dark valleys, children of light!
The heavens are singing today!
Know that our God is walking with us,
straightening the journey of life.
We sing with the heavens today!

Praise Sentences (Isaiah 49, Matthew 6)

O sing for joy; God cares for us all!
O sing for joy; God cares for us all!

MARCH 6, 2011

Transfiguration Sunday
Deborah Sokolove

COLOR
White

SCRIPTURE READINGS
Exodus 24:12-18; Psalm 99; 2 Peter 1:16-21;
Matthew 17:1-9

THEME IDEAS
The story of Moses' mountain ascent to receive God's
commandments is juxtaposed with the story of Jesus'
mountain ascent when he was transfigured in the midst of
his disciples. The presence of Moses and Elijah on the
mountain with Jesus emphasizes his continuity with the
ongoing story of God's journey with the people of God.
Images of light, of the shining glory of God, suffuse
today's readings. As Jesus is transfigured, his face shining
like the sun, we see a new world in which God establishes
justice and righteousness for all.

INVITATION AND GATHERING
Call to Worship (Exodus 24, Matthew 17)
As God called to Moses from the mountain,
we are called to be God's people.
As Jesus called the disciples to climb with him

to the peak of another mountain,
we are called to follow wherever he leads.
As the disciples stood in awe at the sound of God's voice,
we are called to worship in wonder and praise.

Opening Prayer (Exodus 24, Matthew 17)
Holy One, Light of light, God of all creation,
long ago you showed yourself
to the disciples in Jesus' transfiguration—
his face glowing like a field of daffodils
on a bright, spring morning.
Shine in us, around us, and through us,
that the world may see your glory
in the faces of your people—
faces transfigured in the light of your love. Amen.

PROCLAMATION AND RESPONSE

Prayer of Confession (Exodus 24, Matthew 17)
Though we want to walk with Moses
and see God's holy radiance,
we hide in the mist of our own desires,
unable to perceive the presence of God's grace.
While we want a world of justice and peace,
we walk in clouds of selfishness,
unable to share God's loving-kindness.
Though we want to follow Jesus up the mountain,
we cower in fear,
unable to bear the light of God.

Words of Assurance (Matthew 17)
In the blazing light of God's grace,
Jesus touches us to say,
"Get up and do not be afraid."
In the name of Christ, all is forgiven.
Amen.

Passing the Peace of Christ
>As we share the peace of Christ with one another,
>may the light of Christ shine in you always.
>**And also in you.**

Response to the Word (Exodus 24, Psalm 99,
2 Peter 1, Matthew 17)
>Light of light, True God of true God,
>>as you spoke from the pillar of cloud
>>>to Moses and the people,
>>>>so you spoke from the bright cloud
>>>>>to Jesus and his disciples.
>May your word live through us today,
>>that our world of sorrow
>>>may be transfigured into joy.

THANKSGIVING AND COMMUNION

Offering Prayer
>Luminous Giver of all good things,
>>in your presence, everything is gift.
>Bless these gifts of bread and wine,
>>fruit of the vine and work of human hands,
>>that they may nourish us
>>>for the work of healing your creation,
>>>>in the name of Christ, our light
>>>>>and the light of the world. Amen.

Great Thanksgiving
>Christ be with you.
>>**And also with you.**
>Lift up your hearts.
>>**We lift them up to God.**
>Let us give our thanks to the Holy One.
>>**It is right to give our thanks and praise.**

>It is a right, good, and a joyful thing
>>always and everywhere to give you our thanks,
>>you who created all that is
>>and all that ever shall be.

On the first day of creation, you said,
   "Let there be light," and there was light;
   and you called the light good.
From mountaintops to the deepest valleys,
   in daylight and in the darkest shadows,
   you call us to be your people.

And so, with your people on earth
   and all the great cloud of witnesses in heaven,
   we praise your name
   and join their unending hymn:
   **Holy, holy, holy One, God of power and might,
      heaven and earth are full of your glory.
   Hosanna in the highest. Blessed is the one
      who comes in your holy name.
   Hosanna in the highest.**

Holy are you, and holy is your child, Jesus Christ.
When he went up the mountain with his disciples,
   he stood in the company of Moses and Elijah,
   enveloped in the bright cloud of your presence.
When he saw that his friends were afraid,
   he touched them with compassion,
   freeing them from fear.

On the night in which he gave himself up
(*continue Words of Institution*)
   do this in remembrance of me.

And so, in remembrance of your mighty acts
   in Jesus Christ, we offer ourselves
   in praise and thanksgiving
   as a holy and living sacrifice
   as we proclaim the mystery of faith.
   **Christ has died.
   Christ is risen.
   Christ will come again.**

Pour out your Holy Spirit on us gathered here,
  and on these gifts of bread and wine.
Make them be for us the body and blood of Christ,
  that we may become one with Christ,
  who lived and died and rose to eternal life,
  an eternal blessing for the world.

By your Spirit make us one with Christ,
  one with each other, and one in ministry
  to all the world, until we feast together
  at the heavenly banquet in your eternal realm.
Light of light, True God of true God,
  Spirit of holiness, we praise you now,
  tomorrow, and forevermore.

SENDING FORTH

Benediction (2 Peter 1, Matthew 17)
  Walk in light and truth.
  See the light of Christ in every face.
  Be the light of Christ to all you meet. Amen.

CONTEMPORARY OPTIONS

Gathering Words (Matthew 17)
  On mountaintops and in deep valleys,
  Jesus is the light of the world.
  On busy city streets and on quiet country lanes,
  Jesus is the light of the world.
  At home, at work, at play, and at rest,
  Jesus is the light of the world.
  Let us see one another in the light of Jesus.
—Or—

Gathering Words (Exodus 24, 2 Peter 1)
  A bush burns and is not consumed.
  God is present among us.
  A voice calls out from the clouds.

God is present among us.
A light shines in the darkness,
and the morning star rises in our hearts.
God is present among us.

Praise Sentences (Matthew 17)
Christ is our light and our hope!
Christ is our light and our hope!

MARCH 9, 2011

Ash Wednesday
Bryan Schneider-Thomas

COLOR
Purple

SCRIPTURE READINGS
Joel 2:1-2, 12-17; Psalm 51:1-17;
2 Corinthians 5:20b–6:10; Matthew 6:1-6, 16-21

THEME IDEAS
Our Ash Wednesday scriptures focus upon repentance and preparation. Ash Wednesday is the invitation to a forty-day Lenten journey—a journey of preparation that culminates in the Triduum (the three days beginning on Holy Thursday) and finally in the Easter celebration. The call to repentance is the beginning of this journey. Creating an atmosphere of reflection and devotion serves the intent of Ash Wednesday, as does providing time and space for individual reflection and confession.

INVITATION AND GATHERING

Call to Worship (Joel 2)
Come, young and old.
Sanctify yourselves before the Lord.
We gather to hear the word of God.

Come, and do not delay.
Return to God.
We gather to be in the presence of God.
Come, cry out to God.
Trust in God's mercy.
We gather to find the renewal of our spirit,
as we acknowledge our failings before God.

Opening Prayer (Joel 2)

We turn to you, God of life,
   on this first day of Lent
     as we recall our own mortality.
With hearts torn open by our actions,
   we need your guidance
     and your healing forgiveness.
Ready us to receive your mercy and grace,
   and cleanse us of the ash of human failing,
     that we may embrace the words you speak—
       the words that lead to eternal life. Amen.

PROCLAMATION AND RESPONSE

Prayer of Confession (Psalm 51)

In preparation, present yourselves before God.
Come in your brokenness,
acknowledging where you have fallen short
of God's expectations and your own.
(Pause for silent reflection.)
Have mercy on me, O God,
according to your steadfast love.
My brokenness that hinders me
I lay before you.
Come in your pain,
acknowledging your hurt
and how you have hurt others.
(Pause for silent reflection.)
Do not cast me away from your presence,
or take your Holy Spirit from me.

All the pain I have in my life,
that which I have caused and that which I feel,
I lay before you.
Come in your weakness,
acknowledging your lack of strength and confidence
to do what is right.
(Pause for silent reflection.)
Have mercy on me, O God,
according to your steadfast love.
The weakness that holds me captive
I lay before you.
Come in your fear,
acknowledging your failure to speak up for justice.
(Pause for silent reflection.)
Do not cast me away from your presence,
or take your Holy Spirit from me.
My fear that binds me
I lay before you.
Come in your hesitancy,
acknowledging your resistance to God's call.
(Pause for silent reflection.)
Have mercy on me, O God,
according to your steadfast love.
My hesitancy in doing your will
I lay before you.
Come in your sinfulness,
acknowledging what you have done
and left undone.
(Pause for silent reflection.)
Create in me a clean heart, O God,
and put a new and right spirit within me.
The sin, which eats at my heart
and leaves me lifeless, I lay before you.
All that we are, all that we have done,
all that we confess, we lay before you, God.
Relieve us from this burden. Amen.

Words of Assurance (Joel 2)

Joel reminds us that God is gracious and merciful,
slow to anger and abounding in steadfast love.
With great mercy, God relents from punishing.
In God's grace, know that you are forgiven.
In God's grace, know that you are forgiven.
In God's mercy, know that you are made new.
In God's mercy, know that you are made new.
In God's love, know that you are made whole.
In God's love, know that you are made whole.

Introduction to the Word (Psalm 51, 2 Corinthians 5)

We entreat you on behalf of Christ,
be reconciled to God.
Speak, O Lord, and we will listen!
In our innermost heart,
may your wisdom dwell.

—Or—

Introduction to the Word (Psalm 51, 2 Corinthians 5)

Hear the word of God.
Speak to us the word!
We listen with open hearts
and contrite spirits.

Response to the Word (Psalm 51, 2 Corinthians 5)

Together we have heard the word of God.
Accept God's grace, that our hearing will not be in vain.
Create in us a clean heart, O God,
and put a right spirit within us.

THANKSGIVING AND COMMUNION

Invitation to the Offering

(This may be an opportunity to collect an offering that is something other than money. You may wish to invite people to write their sins, confessions, Lenten commitments, or other appropriate words on small slips of paper. Give instructions on this prior to the beginning of worship so that the congregation has time to

think, pray, and respond. These slips could then be collected and offered to God. If time, space, and safety permit, burn the paper and use the ash later in the service for the imposition of the ashes.)

Tonight our offering to God is a written sign of our *(sins/confessions/commitment).* Place these signs in the offering plate as it passes. The God of grace and mercy will hear your cry.

(Alternatively, if you are encouraging people to take on a Lenten discipline, this may be a good time to pass out tokens of this discipline, such as a small cross, to the congregation.)

Typically, our offering to God focuses on the money we give, but tonight (*today*) we ask you to look at your offering as the next forty days. During these days, you are invited to take on a Lenten discipline—a devotion to God. As a reminder of this offering, we encourage you to take a token of this discipline from the offering plate and carry it with you throughout Lent.

Offering Prayer

Almighty God,
>   our lives are an offering to you.
Tonight we offer our naked and honest selves,
>   for you delight not only in praise
>   but also in repentance.
Tonight we offer our failings and faults,
>   for you desire not only glory
>   but also confession of our sorrow and sin.
Lord of Life,
>   take the whole of our offering tonight,
>   for you have the power to make it beautiful
>   in your sight. Amen.

Imposition of Ashes (2 Corinthians)

(A traditional part of Ash Wednesday worship is to make the sign of the cross with ash upon the forehead of each worshiper. Traditionally, the palms from the preceding Palm Sunday are

burned to create the ash. Ash may be mixed with a bit of olive oil to facilitate the process. They should not be mixed with water. You may wish to provide the option to kneel while receiving the imposition. The person making the mark may say one of the following traditional phrases.)

"Remember that you are dust and to dust
    you will return."
—OR—
"Repent and believe in the gospel."
    —OR—
"Marked with the cross, be reconciled to God.
In death, accept the grace of God.
From the ashes of repentance, God brings new life."

Introduction to the Imposition of Ashes (2 Corinthians 5–6)

The Apostle Paul writes:
"We entreat you on behalf of Christ,
    be reconciled to God.
    For our sake [God] made him to be sin
    who knew no sin,
    so that in him we might become
    the righteousness of God.
As we work together with him,
    we urge you also not to accept
    the grace of God in vain."
Ash is a traditional sign of repentance,
    contrition, and sin.
Tonight the mark of the cross
    is made upon your foreheads in ash:
    a sign of our desire to be reconciled with God.
Come before God.
    We come confessing our sins.
Come before God.
    We come acknowledging our need.
Come before God.
    We come facing our own death.

Come before God.
**We come ready to receive God's forgiveness
and new life.**

SENDING FORTH

Benediction
With the ash of repentance, we have entered Lent.
With contrite hearts, we await our Lord.
Go forth and prepare yourselves
to receive the power of God.

CONTEMPORARY OPTIONS

Gathering Words
Now is the time to prepare yourselves.
This is the place for repentance.
We gather in God's presence.
**We come to the Lord of heaven
to bear our hearts, confess our sins,
and prepare for new life.**

Praise Sentences (Joel 2)
God sounds an alarm and calls us together.
God hears our cry and heals our brokenness.

MARCH 13, 2011

First Sunday in Lent
Bill Hoppe

COLOR
Purple

SCRIPTURE READINGS
Genesis 2:15-17; 3:1-7; Psalm 32; Romans 5:12-19;
Matthew 4:1-11

THEME IDEAS
The central ideas for this first Sunday in Lent are temptation, sin, right and wrong, and how we respond to each. The
familiar story of the temptation and sin of Adam and Eve is
no less relevant today than when it was first told, and Paul
uses this story as a primary foundation for his doctrine of
Christ's atonement for the sins of humankind. The psalmist
sings of the joy and relief of forgiveness, which comes from
acknowledgment and confession. Finally, driven into the
wilderness by the Spirit and armed with only God's word,
Jesus confronts temptation at the end of his forty days and
nights of fasting without yielding to it.

INVITATION AND GATHERING

Call to Worship (Psalm 32)
Happy are those whose sins are forgiven.
Happy are those whose sins are cast away.

Rejoice in the Lord! Be glad!
> **Sing out! Shout for joy!**

Rejoice in the Lord!
> **Rejoice! Amen!**

Opening Prayer (Genesis 2, 3; Psalm 32; Matthew 4)

Holy One,
> we are constantly bombarded
> > with temptations and enticements.

When we yield, when we fail,
> who will help us?

You, Lord, have come to our aid.
You teach us, counsel us, and guide us
> in the ways we should go.

We rejoice in your unfailing love. Amen.

PROCLAMATION AND RESPONSE

Prayer of Confession (Psalm 32)

We keep silent before you, Lord—
> we are afraid to confront our transgressions;
> we are terrified to face the reality of our sin;
> we feel as if the weight of the world
> > were upon our shoulders;
>
> we no longer recognize ourselves
> > or what we have become
> > > as we keep our failings and fears inside.

Help us admit our sins and accept our imperfections.
Why is that simple act so difficult for us?
Why do we hesitate, knowing that you stand ready
> to wash away our guilt?

You are the sanctuary where distress cannot reach us.
In your steadfast love, forgive us.
In your healing caress, cleanse us.
In your Holy Spirit, restore us.
In the name of our Savior, we pray. Amen.

Words of Assurance (Psalm 32)

When distress and anxiety surround us
   like an angry flood,
     our pleas are heard.
The Lord hears the prayers of a faithful heart.
God has become our hiding place,
   our refuge from trouble.
No harm can touch us here.
The Lord wraps us in the arms of salvation.
Shouts of deliverance enfold us.

Passing the Peace of Christ (Romans 5)

Abundant grace is God's gift to us. Out of all proportion
to our wrongdoing, we receive grace and forgiveness from
God's amazing love, revealed to us in Christ Jesus. Share
this love, so freely given to us, with one another.

Response to the Word (Genesis 2, 3; Matthew 4; Romans 5)

The Tempter appears to us in many guises and always in
the manner to which we are most vulnerable. We know
right from wrong, yet we become complicit with the
Tempter when we use the word of the Lord to justify our
disobedience and transgressions. Yet in Christ, our sin is
overcome with a single act of obedience to God: one just
act has brought acquittal and life to all.

THANKSGIVING AND COMMUNION

Offering Prayer (Matthew 4)

In the hour of his temptation, when Jesus hungered,
   he knew from where his sustenance came:
     "One does not live by bread alone,
     but by every word that comes
     from the mouth of God."
Lord,
   from the abundance of your grace,
     your word has provided all that we need.
All that we have is yours.

Receive the offering of our hands
 and the gratitude of our hearts.
In the name of our Savior we pray. Amen.

SENDING FORTH

Benediction or Words of Assurance (Romans 5)

Though we were condemned, we have found pardon.
 Though death held dominion over our lives,
 God's grace and gift of righteousness
 now lives and reigns within us.
We are free. We are forgiven. We are alive in Christ!
 Amen!

CONTEMPORARY OPTIONS

Gathering Words (Psalm 32)

The eyes of God are upon us.
 The Lord will guide us.
God will keep us safe.
 No harm can touch us.

Praise Sentences (Psalm 32)

Shout for joy! Sing out! Sing aloud!
Women, men, everyone: Rejoice! Be glad!
Rejoice in the Lord!

MARCH 20, 2011

Second Sunday in Lent
Mary J. Scifres

COLOR

Purple

SCRIPTURE READINGS

Genesis 12:1-4a; Psalm 121; Romans 4:1-5, 13-17;
John 3:1-17

THEME IDEAS

Blessed or born again, we are called God's children for the
purpose of blessing others. Abraham and the Hebrew
people are given a special blessing, that they may be a
blessing for all the families of the earth. Reminding
Nicodemus that he has come to offer eternal life for all
who believe, Jesus invites the faithful Jew into new life
and a new relationship with God. So often, our Judeo-
Christian tradition has been one of exclusion and judgment. Today's passages are often misused to exclude by
showing how unique or special are Jews and Christians.
Yet scripture challenges God's followers to use our unique
lives of faith to bless all the world's peoples. Jesus came
not to exclude but to throw open the door, so that all may
walk into God's waiting arms.

INVITATION AND GATHERING

Call to Worship (Psalm 121, John 3)

Lift up your eyes and see.
>   **The God of heaven and earth welcomes us here.**

Open your minds and trust.
>   **God's protective help is everywhere.**

Lift your hearts and believe.
>   **God so loves the world that all can be saved.**

Opening Prayer (Genesis 12, Psalm 121)

Sheltering God,
>   hold us close to your heart
>   as we worship and pray.

Be the shade at our right hand,
>   protecting us from the glare of confusion
>   and the heat of temptation.

Be our steady guide
>   as we come into this sacred time
>   of worship and reflection,
>   that we may hear and understand
>   your word in our lives.

Be our strong support
>   as we go out into the world,
>   that we may be a blessing
>   for the people of this earth.

PROCLAMATION AND RESPONSE

Prayer of Confession (Genesis 12, John 3)

Savior God,
>   guide us into the truth
>   of your generous love.

When we try to exclude others from your promise,
>   forgive us and open our hearts
>   to be as generous and open with others
>   as your Spirit is with us.

When we think ourselves righteous
>   or judge others to be condemned,

67

forgive us and soften our hearts
 to be as gentle and loving
  as Jesus the Christ was
  when he walked upon this earth.
Guide us to be people of true faith,
 blessed to be a blessing,
 born anew to share your salvation with all.
In Christ's name, we pray. Amen.

—Or—

Prayer of Confession (John 3)

Jesus, Rabbi, Savior God,
 we come to you in the secret night of our sins
  and ask for your forgiveness.
Signs of your loving forgiveness
 and merciful salvation abound around us,
  yet we come seeking assurance
  of the new life you offer.
As we open our hearts to you,
 blow through our lives with your forgiveness,
  that we might be born anew.
(A time of silence may follow.)

Words of Assurance (John 3)

Know this: God so loved and loves the world
 that God sent Jesus into the world,
 not to condemn, but to save.
We shall not perish,
 for in Christ, we are given eternal life.
Rejoice! We are forgiven and made new
 in the Spirit of God!

Passing the Peace of Christ (Genesis 12, John 3)

Born anew in God's Spirit, let us bless one another with signs of love and reconciliation. Share the peace that passes all understanding as we greet one another this morning.

Prayer of Preparation or
Response to the Word (Genesis 12, John 3)
God of ages past and days to come,
    open our hearts to the message of your love.
Bless us with your truth and wisdom,
    that we might be a blessing to others,
    revealing your promises to the world
        in our words and actions.
Blow through our lives with your Spirit,
    that we may be born anew,
    enlivened to blow through the world
        with love and faith for all to see.
In Christ's name, we pray. Amen.

THANKSGIVING AND COMMUNION

Invitation to the Offering (Genesis 12)
As God has blessed us, remember that our blessings come
so that we might bless others. Let us share this promise as
we open our hearts and share our abundance with a
world in need of God's blessings.

Offering Prayer (Genesis 12, John 3)
Bless these gifts,
    even as you bless our lives, O God.
Through our offerings of time, talent, and wealth,
    may your name be made great in the world.
May your blessing be shared with all in need,
    and may Christ's saving love be revealed
        to all the ends of the earth.

SENDING FORTH

Benediction (Genesis 12, John 3)
Go now, as Abraham once went,
onto the path that God reveals.
    We go forth to bless and share,
    to give and love.
Go with God's blessing,
for you are indeed children of the Spirit!

CONTEMPORARY OPTIONS

Gathering Words (John 3)

Listen, the wind is blowing where it will.
   Blow, Holy Spirit, with wisdom and truth.
Listen, God is speaking still.
   Blow, Holy Spirit, with wisdom and truth.
Listen, God's Spirit is in this place.
   Blow, Holy Spirit, with wisdom and truth.

Praise Sentences (Psalm 121)

Lift up your eyes.
   God is the help and hope of our lives!
Lift up your eyes.
   God is the help and hope of our lives!

MARCH 27, 2011

Third Sunday in Lent
Joanne Carlson Brown

COLOR
Purple

SCRIPTURE READINGS
Exodus 17:1-7; Psalm 95; Romans 5:1-11; John 4:5-42

THEME IDEAS
Hope can be in short supply when you are wandering in the desert not knowing if or when you will arrive at your destination; when you are a woman shunned by your community; when your community is not listening to God's voice. But hope takes many forms—water in the desert, living water at a well, encountering a person who changes your life, knowing a God who has created everything and loves all that has been created.

INVITATION AND GATHERING

Call to Worship (Psalm 95, Romans 5)
O come, let us sing to our God
and make a joyful noise
to the rock of our salvation.
We lift our hearts and voices
in joy and thanksgiving
for being here together
in the presence of our beloved God.

Come, let us worship this amazing God,
for we belong to God.
We will listen for God's word
and live in the hope it inspires.

Opening Prayer (Exodus 17, Romans 5, John 4)

Loving and caring God,
we come this morning in hope—
hope that will sustain us in our trying times,
our lonely times, our doubting times.
Refresh us this morning with the living water
of your presence and love.
Open us to the possibilities of friendship—
the possibilities of encountering you
in unexpected ways,
the possibilities of seeing the miraculous
in everyday life. Amen.

PROCLAMATION AND RESPONSE

Prayer of Confession (Exodus 17)

Patient and ever-faithful God,
we come to you this morning
confessing that we can be a grumpy
and unsatisfied people.
When things are not perfect in our eyes,
we murmur and complain,
and grumble and doubt.
We lose hope in the people around us
and, even worse, we lose hope in you.
We challenge instead of accept.
We put you to the test
rather than trust your caring love.
Forgive our doubts and complaining.
Forgive our loss of hope.
Let your healing, life-giving waters pour over us.
Restore our souls. Amen.

Words of Assurance (Exodus 17, Romans 5, John 4)

Our hope and assurance
rest in God's unfailing love and forgiveness.
Open your hearts and minds and souls
that the healing waters
of God's never-ending love and forgiveness
may flow into and over you.
Know that in this love and forgiveness
you have encountered the living God.

Passing the Peace (Romans 5, John 4)

Let us greet one another with words of hope—words that come from the wellspring of love flowing within us because of our encounter with the living Christ.

Response to the Word (Romans 5, John 4)

For the word of hope that pours over us
like living water,
for the word of grace that leads us to encounter
the living Christ,
we offer you our thanks, O God.

THANKSGIVING AND COMMUNION

Invitation to the Offering (Romans 5, John 4)

We are called to live in hope and to share this hope with the world. Let us offer thanks to God for all God has given us by sharing generously of ourselves and of our resources. Through our gifts, may all experience the hope to be found in our life-giving God.

Offering Prayer (Exodus 17, John 4)

Life-giving God,
we offer you ourselves and our resources.
Use us and our gifts,
that we may be water bearers
to a world thirsty for love,
for meaning, for justice, and for hope.

May all your people encounter fullness of life
through the love of Christ, which lives within us.
Amen.

SENDING FORTH

Benediction (Exodus 17, Romans 5, John 4)
We have encountered the living God
through the love of the living Christ.
We have been refreshed by living water.
Go now to live in the hope this encounter inspires.
Be water bearers to a dry and parched world,
knowing that the God of love and hope
goes before you and with you always. Amen.

CONTEMPORARY OPTIONS

Gathering Words (Exodus 17, Romans 5, John 4)
Come and see...water gushing from a rock.
Come and see...someone who knows you
through and through.
Come and see...hope alive, right here, right now.
Come and see...then give God thanks and praise.
We come to worship the God of life and love.

Praise Sentences (Psalm 95)
Sing praise to God!
Our God is a great God!
Come worship and kneel before God our maker!

APRIL 3, 2011

Fourth Sunday in Lent
One Great Hour of Sharing

B. J. Beu

COLOR

Purple

SCRIPTURE READINGS

1 Samuel 16:1-13; Psalm 23; Ephesians 5:8-14;
John 9:1-41

THEME IDEAS

Vision focuses these readings. God does not see as mortals
see. God instructs Samuel not to be influenced by human
beauty in finding Saul's successor to the throne. The
psalmist teaches us to see God's presence even in the
darkest valley. Paul encourages us to be children of light
and to do the works of the day, that Christ's light may
shine on us. And in John's Gospel, Jesus heals a man born
blind, while the religious leaders are blinded by their pre-
conceived ideas that physical blindness is a punishment
for human sin. To see as we are called to see, God must be
our vision.

INVITATION AND GATHERING

Call to Worship (Psalm 23, Ephesians 5)
Sleeper, awake! Christ's light is shining.
We are children of light.
Put aside the works of darkness.
In the Lord, we are light.
We are children of light.
Even in the darkest valley, God's glory sustains us.
We are children of light.
Sleeper, awake! Christ's light is shining.
We are children of light.

Opening Prayer (Psalm 23, Ephesians 5)
God of light,
be our vision,
that we may see through your eyes—
eyes that see the world as it can be
even in times of deepest despair;
eyes that perceive your light
even in the darkest valleys;
eyes that observe your grace and mercy
even amidst suffering and death.
Help us live as children of light,
that others may see in our living
the reflection of your glory,
through Christ, who shines in our lives.

PROCLAMATION AND RESPONSE

Prayer of Confession (1 Samuel 16, John 9)
Forgive us in your mercy, O God—
when we fear what we do not understand;
when we let prejudice blind us;
when we cling to feelings of superiority;
when we refuse to witness your healing
in those we think ill of.
Free us from all blindness,
that we may behold your glory
and reflect your light for all to see. Amen.

Words of Assurance (Psalm 23)
The One who shepherds Israel is our shepherd.
The One who leads us through the darkest valleys
anoints us with love,
fills our cup to overflowing,
and brings us goodness and mercy
all the days of our lives.

Response to the Word (Ephesians 5, John 9)
The Word made flesh is the light of the world, shining on
us each and every day of our lives. Hear the word, see the
light, and bear fruit as children of light.

THANKSGIVING AND COMMUNION

Offering Prayer (Psalm 23)
Loving Shepherd,
we come to you in thanks
for giving us rest in green pastures,
for offering us drink beside still waters,
for restoring our souls;
we offer you our love
for walking with us
through valleys of death and despair,
for feeding us from your table,
for saving us from those who would harm us.
As grateful sheep of your pasture,
we rejoice in your goodness and mercy
and we offer these gifts of gratitude,
that we may share with others
the blessings we have received
from your hand.

SENDING FORTH

Benediction (Ephesians 5, John 9)
Christ's light shines in our darkness.
We will see as children of light.

Christ's love illumines our path.
We will love as children of light.
Christ's spirit leads us from death to life.
We will live as children of light.
Thanks be to God.

CONTEMPORARY OPTIONS

Gathering Words (Isaiah 42)
Wake up, sleepy heads.
It's too early. Can't you turn the lights down?
Christ's light is shining. It's time to wake up.
A few more minutes would be great.
Does it have to be this bright?
Christ is the light of the world.
Does that make us children of the light?
You know it does. Now, wake up!
Worship the lord of light.
We worship the light of the world!

Praise Sentences (Ephesians 5)
Jesus is the light of the world!
Worship the lord of light.
Rejoice in our God, you children of light.
Worship the lord of light.
Jesus is the light of the world!

APRIL 10, 2011

Fifth Sunday in Lent
Girl Scout Sunday
Laura Jaquith Bartlett

COLOR

Purple

SCRIPTURE READINGS

Ezekiel 37:1-14; Psalm 130; Romans 8:6-11; John 11:1-45

THEME IDEAS

The Spirit of God brings new life! This theme dances through today's readings. While the Sundays in Lent are not counted toward the forty days of Lent itself, most congregations lean toward repentance during the Sundays of this season. Into our sense of despair comes God's promise of resurrection! Two of the Bible's most startling stories of death-turned-to-life are put together this week, along with a short commentary from Romans, reminding us that the One, "who raised Christ from the dead will give life to your mortal bodies also. . . ." As an Easter people, this is life-giving news, indeed!

INVITATION AND GATHERING

Call to Worship (Ezekiel 37, John 11)
Can these bones live?
Only God knows.

Can these people wake up to the good news?
Only God knows.
Can this church be revitalized?
Only God knows.
Come, Holy Spirit, and breathe your life
into our worship this hour.
**Unbind us and set us free
to proclaim our faith as your Easter people!**

Opening Prayer *(Ezekiel 37, John 11)*
God of new life,
    free us from the bonds
        that keep us tethered
            to the ways of death.
Where there is hopelessness,
    breathe into us the breath of hope.
Where our lives have become dry and brittle,
    blow through us with the winds of change.
Lead us from the depths of despair
    into the joy of your resurrection.
Put your Spirit into the very core of our being,
    that we might live, and live abundantly,
        as people of faith. Amen.

PROCLAMATION AND RESPONSE

Prayer of Confession *(Ezekiel 37, John 11)*
God of the resurrection,
    we do not always live as Easter people.
Too often, we find ourselves distracted
    by the rattling of dry bones.
It is so easy to forget your gift of living water
    when we are surrounded by dust, despair,
        and desert.
In the midst of death,
    we cannot envision the way of life;
    we lack the ability to see beyond
        the bondage of hopelessness.

Come free us, O God!
Heal us, Christ Jesus!
Loosen the bonds
   that prevent us from entering new life
     in your Spirit.
We long for Easter.
Come free us!

Words of Assurance (John 11, Romans 8)

Jesus said, "Unbind him, and let him go."
The One who raised Lazarus from the dead
   also holds the power to free us from sin and death.
The Spirit dwells in us and gives us new life.

Passing the Peace of Christ (Ezekiel 37)

Shaking hands is an ancient ritual that is too often mean-
ingless, cold, shallow, and lifeless. Not here! Shake hands
with one another right now as if you are passing on new
life. Can these dry bones live? Answer the question with
your handshake, by offering new life and new hope to the
people around you.

Response to the Word (John 11)

*(Written for two voices, this response should flow quickly and
is designed to follow a reading of John 11:1-45 without intro-
duction or commentary.)*
Cold and dark.
   Tomb of death.
All hope gone.
   Stench of despair.
Tears flowing.
   Weeping, crying, wailing.
Grief all around.
   Deep sadness, bitter anger.
Where were you?
   Why didn't you come?
You could have stopped this!
   You could have made a difference!
If only.

If only.
No death; if only.
No death; do you believe?
If only; do I believe?
No death!
Do you believe?
Unbind him, and let him go.
No death!
If only.
We believe.
If only.
(in unison, after a pause)
Unbind us, and let us go!
Unbind us, and let us go!

THANKSGIVING AND COMMUNION

Offering Prayer (Ezekiel 37)
God of life,
    you have given us our very existence.
Even when we are dried up
    and feel only hopelessness and despair,
    you enliven us with your Spirit
        and raise us up once again.
With grateful hearts
    we offer you our gifts, our service, our selves.
Accept our offerings, O God.
Breathe into us
    and bless us with your grace and love,
    that we might choose the way of life
        as we journey toward the resurrection
            and beyond. Amen.

SENDING FORTH

Benediction (Romans 8, John 11)
Know that Jesus Christ is waiting to unbind you
    and free you for joyful service in the world.

The Spirit that raised Christ from the dead
   is the same Spirit that dwells in you,
   giving you new life.
Go with the peace of God and live! Amen.

CONTEMPORARY OPTIONS

Gathering Words (Ezekiel 37)

(Congregation is seated.)

Voice 1:   Get up, all you people!

People: **We're tired and lifeless. We can't get up.**

Voice 1:   C'mon, up and at 'em! Get up and get with it!

People: **It's too difficult. There's too much despair, too much pain in the world.**

Voice 2:   There is never too much despair for God. Feel God's Spirit blowing over you.

People: **Could that be the breath of hope we feel?**

Voice 2:   With God, new life is always available! Get up; you can do it!

(Congregation stands.)

People: **Let's praise the God of resurrection!**

Praise Sentences (Romans 8)

The Spirit of God dwells in you!
When you set your mind on the Spirit,
   there is life and peace.
The Spirit of God dwells in you!
The One who raised Christ from the dead
   will give you life.
The Spirit of God dwells in you!

APRIL 17, 2011

Palm/Passion Sunday
Marcia McFee

COLOR
Purple

PALM SUNDAY READINGS
Psalm 118:1-2, 19-29; Matthew 21:1-11

PASSION SUNDAY READINGS
Isaiah 50:4-9a; Psalm 31:9-16; Philippians 2:5-11;
Matthew 26:14–27:66 (27:11-54)

THEME IDEAS
This last Sunday in Lent heralds the triumphal entry into
Jerusalem with Jesus the liberator. This Sunday also ushers in the beginning of Holy Week and what feels like de-
feat as we face the consequences of standing up to unjust
authority. While it is difficult to move so quickly from joy
to sorrow, a good symbol can help us make this transition. The palms that are waved at the beginning of the
service become the sign of our "letting go" into the sorrow of the events of the week to come. Encouraged by the
steadfast love of God expressed in the scriptures, this is a
Sunday to stand up together with Jesus even in the face
of adversity.

INVITATION AND GATHERING

Call to Worship (Psalm 118, Matthew 21)

(Needed: one liturgist, five readers, two acolytes, one gong &
player, ten or so youth, and many children with palms. In a call
and response fashion, the liturgist reads the unmarked words
while the congregation reads the bolded words. Only these parts
of the script need to be in the program.)

Liturgist:	When they had come near Jerusalem and had reached Bethphage, at the Mount of Olives, Jesus sent two disciples ahead, saying to them, "Go into the village ahead of you, and immediately you will find a donkey tied, and a colt with her; untie them and bring them to me. If anyone says anything to you, just say this, 'The Lord needs them.' And he will send them immediately."
People:	**Give thanks to the Lord, for God is good. God's steadfast love endures forever.**
Liturgist:	The disciples went and did as Jesus had directed them; they brought the donkey and the colt, and put their cloaks on them, and he sat on them. A very large crowd spread their cloaks on the road, and others cut branches from the trees and spread them on the road.
(Gong sounds)	
Reader 1:	*(from the back)* Open the gates of righteousness; I will enter and give thanks to God.
Reader 2:	*(from the back)* This is the gate of the Lord through which the righteous may enter.
Readers 1&2:	I will give you thanks, for you answered me; you have become my salvation.

Musical Offering (e.g., a choir may sing the choral introit "The Gates of the City.")

(Call to Worship, Continued)

    (Gong sounds)

Reader 3:   *(from the altar as the ten youths bring cloths down the center aisle and place them on the altar)*
The stone the builders rejected
 has become the capstone;
the Lord has done this,
and it is marvelous in our eyes.

All Readers: *(from around the congregation, randomly, overlapping each other)*
This is the day the Lord has made;
let us rejoice and be glad in it!

(Gong sounds)

Reader 4:   *(from the baptismal font)*
O Lord, save us;
O Lord, grant us success.

(Acolytes come forward with the light)

Reader 4:   The crowds that went ahead of Jesus and that followed him were shouting:

People: **Hosanna to the Son of David!**
Blessed is the One who comes
   in the name of the Lord.
Hosanna in the highest heaven!

Reader 5:   *(from the front center aisle, indicating to acolytes as they pass)*
The Lord is God,
and God has given us light.
(pause as the candles are lit)
With boughs in hand, join in the festal
procession up to the horns of the altar.
When he entered Jerusalem, the whole city
was in turmoil, asking, "Who is this?"
The crowds were saying, "This is the
prophet Jesus from Nazareth in Galilee."

People: **Give thanks to the Lord, for God is good.**
          God's steadfast love endures forever!
All Readers: You are my God, and I will give you thanks;
          you are my God and I will exalt you.

Processional Hymn (e.g., "Hosanna, Loud Hosanna")
*(All persons should have palms to wave from their seats. The
children process with palms, led by banners, ribbons on sticks,
whatever makes a colorful and festive entrance.)*

Unison Prayer of Confession (Matthew 21, Psalm 118)
O God,
   we stand at the gate,
      hesitant and uncertain;
   we are reluctant to answer your invitation;
   we are slow to embark on the journey
      toward your reign.
Forgive us, we pray.
Grant us the help we need to be your people—
   the courage to join you in the procession;
   the selflessness to lay our cloaks before you;
   the freedom to lift our palms to your glory;
   and the knowledge that by your grace
      we are forgiven. Amen.

Assurance of Pardon
Hear this good news!
The procession is ever moving forward.
We can join at any moment.
The invitation still stands!
In the name of Jesus Christ, you are forgiven!
   In the name of Jesus Christ, you are forgiven!
   Glory to God! Amen!

PROCLAMATION AND RESPONSE

Prayer for Illumination (Isaiah 50:4)
God of Courage,
   give us wisdom,

that we may sustain the weary
　　with our words.
As we speak,
　　help us also to listen.
　　Amen.

Response to the Word (Isaiah 50, Psalm 31)
Our God helps us!
　　We stand up together.
Our God is gracious.
　　We put our trust in the Lord.
God's face shines upon us.
　　We find salvation in God's steadfast love.
　　Alleluia! Alleluia! Amen!

THANKSGIVING AND COMMUNION

Offering Prayer (Philippians 2)
Name above all names,
　　as you emptied yourself for others,
　　we offer ourselves and these gifts
　　　　as a sign of our hope in your reign.
Where there is death, bring life.
Where there is sorrow, bring joy.
Where there is injustice, bring courage for change.
　　Amen.

Ritual of Passion (Matthew 27:11-54)
*(As the Matthew text is read, play meditative music under-
neath. Invite people to bring their palm branches to the chancel
and lay them on the steps or altar where they will wither
throughout Holy Week. The invitation to this action should
highlight the move from triumphal entry with the waving of
palms to a much more somber mood as the week progresses.)*

SENDING FORTH

Benediction (Matthew 27:54)
"Truly this man Jesus was God's Son."
As disciples of Jesus, truly you are God's children.
Go into this week with the knowledge
    that resurrection will come,
    even when it seems there is no tomorrow.
Be blessed and be a blessing,
    with the courage to stand with those in need.
In the name of the Creator, Redeemer, and Sustainer.
Amen.

CONTEMPORARY OPTIONS

Gathering Words (Psalm 118)
Open the gates!
    Give us courage to walk through!
Lay down the cloaks.
    We mark the journey to Love's reign.
Lift up the branches!
    Let us boldly proclaim God's peace!

Passion Sentences (Psalm 31)
Grief wastes me.
    Scorn surrounds me.
There is scheming against me.
    My strength fails.
But your face shines.
    I will trust in you.
And your love endures.
    I will trust in you.

APRIL 21, 2011

Holy Thursday
Hans Holznagel

COLOR

Purple

SCRIPTURE READINGS

Exodus 12:1-4 (5-10), 11-14; Psalm 116:1-4, 12-19;
1 Corinthians 11:23-26; John 13:1-17, 31b-35

THEME IDEAS

These readings, depicting the moment before Jesus' persecution, crucifixion, and resurrection, contain familiar
high drama: death and deliverance, blood as sign and
symbol, shared food weighted with meaning. But they
also stress something unfamiliar and countercultural in
today's individualized world: communal caring that tran-
scends personal and family boundaries. "If a household
is too small for a whole lamb, it shall join its closest neighbor in obtaining one," Exodus instructs. "Wash one another's feet," Jesus commands. "Just as I have loved you,
you also should love one another." Even Paul's famous
words of the Lord's Supper are set within a larger exhor-
tation of right practice and relationship within the community of faith.

INVITATION AND GATHERING

Call to Worship (John 13)

From busy weekday lives
  we pause this hour, gathered as friends,
  to remember Jesus' last earthly night
    with his disciples.
May we listen for God's invitations
  to personal discipleship and service;
  to communion with one another
    and with the Holy One.
Let us prepare our hearts and minds
  to worship God.

Opening Prayer (Exodus 12, John 13)

Holy God,
  remind us on this special day
    of the many ways we know you:
      as strong deliverer,
      as humble servant,
      as the One who bids us love one another,
        that the world might know you.
Lead us not only to the beauty of solitary reflection
  but also to community, as we remember together
    your words and your example.
In Christ's name, we pray. Amen.

PROCLAMATION AND RESPONSE

Prayer of Confession (Exodus 12, 1 Corinthians 11, John 13)

God of service and abundance,
  on this night of holy meals,
    we are reminded that we ought to love
      and share with one another.
We confess that your ways
  are not always our ways.
When we drift toward isolation and indifference,
  may we remember this night of communion

and your ever new commandment of love.
May our love and sharing
be signs of hope for the world. Amen.

Words of Assurance (Psalm 116)

The Lord has heard our voices and our supplications. God has loosed our bonds. Know that when we fall short, God hears our prayers and frees us for lives of gratitude and service. In Christ we are forgiven. Let the whole church say amen.
Amen.

Response to the Word (1 Corinthians 11)

May the word opened, like bread broken, nourish us for God's service. Thanks be to God! Amen.

THANKSGIVING AND COMMUNION

Invitation to the Offering (Psalm 116:12-14)

To the question, "What shall I return to the LORD for all [God's] bounty to me," the psalmist answers: "I will lift up the cup of salvation and call on the name of the LORD, I will pay my vows to the LORD in the presence of all [God's] people." As we prepare to lift the cup, let us offer thanksgiving through our tithes and offerings. Praise be to God.

Offering Prayer (Psalm 116, John 13)

We offer these gifts, O God,
with joy and thanks.
May they strengthen your church
for acts of love and service,
in Jesus' name. Amen.

Invitation to Communion (John 13)

We are gathered as disciples, and tonight Jesus reveals himself to us. He is the master teacher who unexpectedly washes our feet, as would a servant. He has led us triumphantly into Jerusalem, and yet he speaks of going where we cannot go, of being broken and poured out for us. We remember him now as he asked us to do, in a communal meal. Whether bewildered that he must depart, sobered before the cross that awaits, or quietly anticipating Sunday's joy, let us center ourselves now—in this moment, connected with those around us—to seek God's presence in the breaking of the bread.

SENDING FORTH

Benediction (John 13)

Jesus said, "I give you a new commandment,
    that you love one another.
Just as I have loved you,
    you also should love one another.
By this everyone will know that you are my disciples,
    if you have love for one another."
Go in peace, then, loving one another
    and loving the world that God so loved. Amen.

CONTEMPORARY OPTIONS

Gathering Words (John 13)

Thursday night is not our usual time to meet.
Something is up.
Why the teacher as a servant?
What of leaving and remembering?
What does this mean?
Jesus, help us understand.

Praise Sentences (Psalm 116)

For all God's bounty, what shall I return?
    I will lift the cup of salvation.
    I will offer thanksgiving.
I will pay my vows to God.
    For God has heard my voice
    and my prayers.
Gracious is God, and righteous!
    Praise God!

APRIL 22, 2011

Good Friday
Shelley Cunningham

COLOR
Black or None

SCRIPTURE READINGS
Isaiah 52:13–53:12; Psalm 22; Hebrews 10:16-25;
John 18:1–19:42

THEME IDEAS
We live in a world that needs Good Friday now as much
as ever. Estrangement, injustice, violence, despair, and
war are but signs of our broken relationships—with God
and with each other. In this service of Tenebrae, the worship space becomes increasingly darkened, signifying that
our move away from God comes not with one sudden rejection, but by everyday small steps: one denial, one betrayal, one insult, one lash at a time. Some of these sins
are in direct defiance of God. Many wound God's people
and, in so doing, pierce God's own heart. In naming our
sins, our part in Christ's death, we realize how much we
need this day—a day when we realize the depth of God's
love for us.

INVITATION AND GATHERING

Opening Prayer (John 19)

Lord,
> our journey ends here,
> > at the foot of your cross.

Darkness is falling.
The crowd is restless.
Our hearts break
> as your cries pierce the night.

Stay with us, Lord.
We need to feel you close.
And when the night is over
> and the journey continues,
> give us the courage
> > to stay with you. Amen.

Litany of Confession (Isaiah 53, John 19)

Surely he has borne our infirmities
and carried our diseases.
> **I am the one who held the nails.**

We accounted him stricken,
struck down by God, and afflicted.
> **I am the one who raised the hammer.**

But he was wounded for our transgressions.
> **I am the one who rolled the dice.**

He was crushed for our iniquities.
> **I am the one who pointed and laughed.**

Upon him was the punishment that made us whole.
> **I am the one for whom he died.**

By his bruises we are healed.
> **Father, forgive me, for I know not what I do.**
> **I need your cross to make me whole.**

Words of Assurance (Hebrews 10)

Even as he hung on the cross,
> Jesus spoke words of love.

To the thief, to his tormentors,
  to a world of sinners, our Lord says,
    "I will remember your sins no more."
For you Jesus carried that cross.
For you Jesus bled and died.
For you Jesus spoke words of love.

PROCLAMATION AND RESPONSE

(Place seven candles on a bare altar. After each word or passage is read, extinguish one candle. It is powerful to accompany each candle with the ringing of a single bell and a slight darkening of the sanctuary or worship space.)

Tenebrae Liturgy

(Tenebrae Response is from Isaiah 53)

First Word

Liturgist: Father, forgive them,
        for they know not what they do.
        (Read Luke 23:32-38)
        And we, like sheep, have gone astray.
People: **We have all turned to our own way.**
(Extinguish first candle)

Second Word

Liturgist: Today, you shall be with me
        in paradise.
        (Read Luke 23:39-43)
        And we, like sheep, have gone astray.
People: **We have all turned to our own way.**
(Extinguish second candle)

Third Word

Liturgist: Woman, mother, behold your son.
        Behold your mother.
        (Read John 19:23-27)
        And we, like sheep, have gone astray.
People: **We have all turned to our own way.**
(Extinguish third candle)

Fourth Word

Liturgist: My God, my God,
             why have you forsaken me?
             (Read Matthew 27:45-49)
             And we, like sheep, have gone astray.
People: **We have all turned to our own way.**
(Extinguish fourth candle)

Fifth Word

Liturgist: I thirst.
             (Read John 19:28-29)
             And we, like sheep, have gone astray.
People: **We have all turned to our own way.**
(Extinguish fifth candle)

Sixth Word

Liturgist: It is finished.
             (Read John 19:30)
             And we, like sheep, have gone astray.
People: **We have all turned to our own way.**
(Extinguish the sixth candle)

Seventh Word

Liturgist: Father, into your hands
             I commit my spirit.
             (Read Luke 23:44-49)
             And we, like sheep, have gone astray.
People: **We have all turned to our own way.**
(Extinguish the seventh candle)

THANKSGIVING AND COMMUNION

Invitation to the Cross (Psalm 22)

*(During this time, worshipers may write down specific sins or
sorrows they wish to bring to God. Place these confessions on a
large wooden cross or upon the altar.)*

Our sins separate us from God. With arms spread wide,
our Lord invites us to return to the source of forgiveness
and grace. Let us bring our sins before God, knowing that
we are not forsaken.

Unison Offering Prayer (John 19)
What can we bring you today, Lord?
Your sacrifice is so great; our gifts seem so meager.
Yet you open your arms to us and accept us as we are.
Take what we have and use it, Lord,
    for the good of your kingdom. Amen.

SENDING FORTH
(There is no benediction on Good Friday. Some congregations completely darken the sanctuary for a moment, removing even the eternal candle to signify the total darkness that enveloped the world when Jesus died. Encourage worshipers to leave in silence.)

CONTEMPORARY OPTIONS

Gathering Words (John 19)
When I am lost and lonely,
    Jesus, remember me.
When worry threatens to crush my spirit,
    Jesus, remember me.
When my words wound someone I love,
    Jesus, remember me.
When I treat others with contempt, disdain, or worse,
    Jesus, remember me.
When you come into your kingdom,
    Jesus, remember me.
    Welcome me home.

Praise Sentences
Jesus died for me today.
    Jesus died for me.
God's love truly knows no limits.
    Praise God for such amazing love!

APRIL 24, 2011

Easter Sunday
Mary J. Scifres

COLOR
White

SCRIPTURE READINGS
Acts 10:34-43; Psalm 118:1-2, 14-24; Colossians 3:1-4;
John 20:1-18 (or Matthew 28:1-10)

THEME IDEAS
On this holiest of days, sorrow is turned into joy. That for
which we have searched is found. This is the day that God
has made, a day of gratitude and praise, a day of rejoicing
and celebrating. But joy and answers to our questions
come after searching and struggling. Peter had to first discern that God shows no partiality, and then spend most
of his ministry trying to convince the early Christians that
Christ's grace is available to all. The psalmist rejoices that
death is not the result of God's harsh punishments; and
yet we know that Jesus took death upon himself as a
means of salvation. Mary weeps and questions before dis-
covering that Jesus has risen and is standing with her in
the garden. And so it is with the Easter story of our lives:
we search, we question, we weep, and we wonder. Then,
Jesus calls us by name, the risen Christ is revealed, hope
is restored, love's triumph is confirmed, and we run forth

with the good news that Christ is alive and living still. Thanks be to God!

INVITATION AND GATHERING

Call to Worship (John 20)
(Begin with a quiet, darkened sanctuary.)
Why are you weeping?
We came seeking joy,
but we are shrouded in darkness.
Whom are you looking for?
We are looking for Jesus,
but the tomb is empty.
Set your mind on things above
and listen for the voice of God.
Our grief is too near.
Listen to the earth. Listen to the sky.
Listen to the voice of God calling ... always calling ...
Mary, Joanna, Michael, Jerry, Leah, Sierra, Ramon ...
Listen ...
(Silence follows as the sanctuary lights are slowly brightened. A choral introit or vocal solo may transition to the next section. "You Are Mine," "Lord of the Dance," or "In the Garden" are all possible selections for quiet reflection. A more traditional proclamation of the resurrection—"Christ Is Risen" or "Up from the Grave He Arose"—is also appropriate. Lights can be brightened gradually to the mood of the sung text or the following litany.)
Set your mind on things above
and hear the heavenly hosts:
Christ has risen!
Christ has risen?
Christ has risen indeed!
Thanks be to God!
(Singing a traditional Easter hymn such as "Christ the Lord Is Risen Today" may follow with full lights.)

Opening Prayer *(John 20)*

Risen Christ,
> we come with songs of joy and words of praise
> > for your powerful love and life-giving grace.

Like those first disciples
> who ran to your empty tomb,
> calm our harried thoughts,
> > that we might hear the message
> > of your resurrection.

Like the grieving Mary
> who searched in the garden,
> reveal yourself to us,
> > that we might know your presence
> > and heed your call.

Transform our doubts into faith,
> that we might be a resurrection community,
> > revealing your loving presence
> > for all the world to see.

PROCLAMATION AND RESPONSE

Prayer of Confession *(Psalm 118, Colossians 3, John 20)*

Mighty God,
> you are the author of life,
> > the power of our salvation.

When our strength fails,
> lift us and carry us onto the path
> > of faithful living.

When, with sinful ways and closed hearts,
> we reject your salvation,
> > set our minds on you,
> > > that we may return to your loving presence
> > > and recognize your guiding light.

When, with fearful souls and angry spirits,
> we choose death and despair,
> > raise us up to new life,
> > > that we may be children of the resurrection,
> > > the Easter people you see in us.

Amen and amen.

Words of Assurance (Acts 10, Psalm 118)

My friends, you shall not die,
for in Christ, you shall live!
For everyone who believes
receives forgiveness of sins
through Christ's name.
Thanks be to God!

Passing the Peace of Christ (John 20)

Go to your brothers and sisters and tell them the good
news: "I have seen the Lord! Thanks be to God!"
"I have seen the Lord! Thanks be to God!"

Response to the Word (John 20)

We are witnesses to all that Christ has done
and is doing.
We know the Easter story,
how in Christ sin and death are no more.
We are witnesses to all that God has promised
and is fulfilling.
We know the Easter story,
how in Christ love and goodness triumph.
We are witnesses to Christ's command,
to preach the good news and testify to God's love.
We will answer Christ's call
and proclaim the risen Christ as Mary did.
Have you seen our God?
We have seen the Lord!
Tell it to everyone you meet.
We have seen the Lord!

THANKSGIVING AND COMMUNION

Invitation to the Offering (Psalm 118, John 20)

We come to God's table, remembering that many will
come to their Easter tables this day and find food for the
journey. We come to God's table, remembering that many
do not know the truth of Christ's resurrection and unending love. We come to God's table, with gratitude and

praise for all that we have and all that we know. We come ready to give and to share, that others may eat and be satisfied, may hear and be reassured, may see and know that God's love is available to all.

Offering Prayer (Acts 10, Colossians 3, John 20)

We lift our gifts to you, O God,
that you may use them to bring new life
to a world trapped in death and despair.
May these gifts become signs of the resurrection
in a world hungry for your touch.
In the name of the risen Christ, we pray. Amen.

Invitation to Communion

We come to God's table, remembering that this is the Easter table of abundance for all. We come to God's table, remembering that this is the table of truth and wisdom for all. We come to God's table, with gratitude and praise for these gracious gifts and Christ's amazing love. We come, knowing that all are welcome and all things are made ready for us in Christ Jesus.

Communion Prayer

Pour out your Holy Spirit
on your servants gathered here
and throughout the earth,
that we may be one on this Easter Sunday
in the power and truth of your life
living within us.
Pour out your loving Spirit
on these gifts of bread and wine,
that they may flow through our bodies and souls
as signs of resurrection and life.
Pour out your powerful Spirit
on all who worship you this day,
that we may be one in ministry
with you and with one another,
and that the world may know
your promise of steadfast love
and everlasting life.

Through your Son, Jesus Christ,
with the Holy Spirit in your holy church,
all honor and glory are yours, almighty God,
both now and forevermore. Amen.

SENDING FORTH

Benediction (John 20)
Why were you weeping?
The world had grown dark.
For whom were you searching?
For one who had died.
Christ is risen and is with us still!
Christ is risen indeed and goes with us now!
Run forth with this news,
for our world is weeping in the dark
and searching for one who is with us still.
Christ is risen! Thanks be to God!

CONTEMPORARY OPTIONS

Gathering Words (Psalm 118)
Give thanks and praise, for God is good!
Christ's love endures forever!
God is our strength and our might.
Christ's love endures forever!
God's love is stronger than death.
Christ's love endures forever!
God has become our salvation and our hope.
Christ's love endures forever!

Praise Sentences (Psalm 118)
Give thanks and praise, for God is good!
Give thanks and praise, for God is good!

—Or—

Praise Sentences (John 20)
Christ has risen!
Christ has risen indeed!

MAY 1, 2011

Second Sunday of Easter
Mary J. Scifres

COLOR
White

SCRIPTURE READINGS
Acts 2:14a, 22-32; Psalm 16; 1 Peter 1:3-9; John 20:19-31

THEME IDEAS
Faith is the critical response to the Easter story. Today's scriptures invite us to respond, even in times of doubt and even in the absence of proof. Believing where we have not seen brings not only blessedness but also the greater invitation to go forth as disciples—disciples sent into the world as God first sent Christ into the world.

INVITATION AND GATHERING

Call to Worship (John 20)
Peace be with you.
And also with you.
As we enter into God's presence,
God calls us by name and invites us to believe.
We believe, O God. Help our unbelief!
As we enter into Christ's resurrection story,
Christ offers us the fullness of life everlasting.

> May we live our faith
> with the fullness of hope and joy!

As we enter into this time of worship,
the Spirit blesses us with a holy calling.

> May we live as disciples,
> serve as Jesus served,
> love as God loves,
> and offer salvation
> as Christ has offered salvation to us.

Opening Prayer or Response to the Word (1 Peter 1, John 20)

Christ, our living hope,
  breathe your Spirit upon us.
Fill us with your faith and love,
  that we may believe and live
    the Easter miracle.
Help us so to believe where we have not seen,
  that others will see in us the living Christ,
    arisen and changing the world even today.
In faith and hope, we pray. Amen.

PROCLAMATION AND RESPONSE

Prayer of Confession (John 20)

Ever-present God,
  we want to know you;
  we want to see you;
  we want to believe and to trust you.
Help our unbelief.
Reveal your presence in our lives
  and in our world.
Guide us to live as children of hope and faith,
  that we may truly experience
    the gift of resurrection.

Words of Assurance (John 20)

Have you resisted belief where you have not seen?
Remember Jesus' promise:

"Blessed are those who have not seen
and yet have come to believe."
Must you still resist belief where there is no proof?
Remember Jesus' challenge:
"Do not doubt but believe!"
Do you find yourself, despite your best efforts,
remaining a doubting Thomas?
Then know this:
God has given us a new birth into a living hope
through the resurrection of Christ from the dead.
God's peace and salvation are ours for the taking.
Thanks be to God!

Passing the Peace of Christ (1 Peter, John 20)
As people with beliefs and doubts, faith and questions, let
us remember that in Christ Jesus we are all reconciled to
God. As forgiven and reconciled sisters and brothers, let
us share signs of peace and hope with one another.
Peace be with you, my sisters and brothers.
And also with you, my friend.

Response to the Word (John 20)
Look around you and see Christ—
living in brothers and sisters gathered here.
Know without a doubt:
We have seen the Lord!
Do not doubt, but believe in Christ's living presence—
here in our hearts and around us in God's world.
Proclaim in faith:
My Lord and my God!
Blessed are you who have not seen
and yet have come to see.
**Blessed are those who have not seen
and yet have come to believe!**

THANKSGIVING AND COMMUNION

Invitation to the Offering (Psalm 16, 1 Peter 1)
God is our chosen portion, the cup of our salvation, the
bread of life. Let us share our gratitude for God's gift of

everlasting presence as we share a portion of God's many abundant gifts with a world in need of the Easter miracle.

Offering Prayer (1 Peter 1, John 20)

Our hearts are glad, O God,
    as we rejoice in your Easter miracle.
We come with gratitude and joy
    for the many gifts you have given,
    but most of all for the gift of Christ
        living amongst us still.
Bless these gifts we return to you,
    that they may become gifts of new life
        to those who are haunted by signs of death:
            despair, poverty, sorrow, violence,
            and loneliness.
Help us live the Easter miracle,
    that we may ourselves be signs
        of resurrection hope for others.
In the name of the risen Christ, we pray. Amen.

Communion Prayer (John 20)

Bless, O God, the breaking of this bread
    and the giving of this cup.
As we share in this miraculous gift
    of Holy Communion,
    pour your Holy Spirit upon us
        and upon these gifts of bread and wine,
        that we may know your peace
            and experience your presence in our lives.
Through your Son, Jesus Christ, we pray. Amen.

SENDING FORTH

Benediction (John 20)

As God sent Jesus into the world,
so Jesus sends us forth this day.
    We go forth with the power of the Holy Spirit
    and the hope of the Easter story.
Go now in peace and love.

May we show and share this miraculous gift
with everyone we meet.

CONTEMPORARY OPTIONS

Gathering Words (John 20)
God's Spirit has called us here. Listen.
The Spirit breathes new life even now. Receive.
Christ offers his miraculous presence. Believe.
God sends us forth as disciples. Serve.

Praise Sentences (Acts 2, John 20)
Deeds of power, signs and wonders!
Christ Jesus has risen from the dead!
Deeds of power, signs and wonders!
Christ Jesus is alive in the world!

MAY 8, 2011

Third Sunday of Easter /
Festival of the Christian
Home/Mother's Day
Sara Dunning Lambert

COLOR

White

SCRIPTURE READINGS

Acts 2:14a, 36-41; Psalm 116:1-4, 12-19;
1 Peter 1:17-23; Luke 24:13-35

THEME IDEAS

The Easter season continues, joining with the celebration
of mothers and families. Today's scriptures look at the gift
of the Holy Spirit in Acts 2 and the unfolding of the Pentecost story. Peter tells us that the Holy Spirit is not just
for the Jews in Judea but for their children, for generations
to come, and for those far away geographically. The people are asked to change their minds in order to change
their hearts and lives—by accepting Christ and baptism.
Along the walk to Emmaus, Luke considers the meaning
of encountering the risen Lord. Will we know him when
we see him? Psalm 116 praises the God who has heard the
voice of God's people. Despite times of trial, distress, and
anguish, God's presence is felt. Underlying all of these

passages is belief in God and building relationships with God and others.

INVITATION AND GATHERING

Call to Worship (Acts 2, Psalm 116, Luke 24)

Loving God, we gather to proclaim the risen Christ.
Whether we find him in worship, in the world,
or along the road of life, you hear our cries
and respond in your steadfast love.
Alleluia, he is come!
We wait and watch for the promise of Christ
to open our eyes; we wait for the Holy Spirit
to descend upon our hearts.
Alleluia, he is come!
As we enter this time of holy reflection,
renewal, and forgiveness, we seek the hope
of the early church, the faith of the disciples,
and the love of Jesus.
Alleluia, he is come!
Amen.
Amen.

Opening Prayer (Acts 2, Psalm 116, Luke 24)

Holy One,
we wait for your presence
to stir among us this day.
As we walk toward faith,
may we open our eyes
and place our trust in you.
Together, we come with joy
to praise and worship you,
knowing that your love
is ours to receive.

PROCLAMATION AND RESPONSE

Prayer of Confession (Acts 2, Luke 24)
Parent of us all,
we know your promise of love is waiting;
we understand the Holy Spirit is your gift to all;
we hear the message of Christ's sacrifice.
Yet, like willful children,
we need the loving arms of our Mother
to gather us into her arms when we disobey;
to teach us once again
that we have fallen short
of her expectations.
We try to repent.
We try to change our minds,
to change our lives.
Help us believe once again,
through your love and forgiveness,
that we may see Christ
in those around us and before us.

Words of Assurance (Acts 2, Luke 24)
Let those who love the Lord
feel the forgiveness of Christ,
as given to us by God and the Holy Spirit.
Open your eyes and see the fulfillment
of God's promised salvation.

Passing the Peace of Christ (Mother's Day: Luke 24)
Today, as we celebrate those who have been mothers to us, we recognize the importance of those who nurture and support us in our journeys of faith. Greet those around you with warmth and motherly love as you share the peace of Christ with one another.

Response to the Word (Acts 2, Luke 24, Psalm 116)
As we travel our own roads, Lord,
we look for your living word
and listen for the Holy Spirit

that rushes through our hearts.
May we learn to praise your name always. Amen.

THANKSGIVING AND COMMUNION

Invitation to the Offering
(Festival of the Christian Home: Acts 2, Luke 24)
Together we are the family of God. As such, we support
one another with our gifts—monetary, spiritual, physical,
and emotional. We must care for those in this church, in
our homes, in our community, in our workplaces, and in
our world. Consider the gifts you have been given cus-
tody of during this lifetime, and make a commitment to
share those gifts with God's family. When you see the
risen Lord, how can you not want to share his love with
all? Give as you are able, knowing each gift is worthy in
God's eyes.

Offering Prayer (Acts 2, Luke 24)
God of grace,
    accept our offerings of love
        and our commitment to work for your people.
May our offering show our acceptance
    of your many gifts,
    and may they be offerings of hospitality
        to travelers along our way.

SENDING FORTH

Benediction (Acts 2, Luke 24)
Walk the road of life in faith and love.
    We walk in the footsteps of the risen Lord!
Change your minds; change your hearts;
change your lives.
    We accept the challenge; we accept the Word;
    we accept Christ.
Amen.

CONTEMPORARY OPTIONS

Gathering Words (Acts 2, Luke 24, Psalm 116)

We gather to greet the risen Lord.
Alleluia, he is come!
The Holy Spirit descends upon our hearts.
The promise of grace is for all!
God be with us as we journey along the road.
We will call on the Lord as long as we live!

Praise Sentences (Acts 2, Psalm 116)

Christ is risen! Alleluia!
The gift of the Holy Spirit is given to all—
near and far, young and old,
believers and nonbelievers!
We will sing of God's steadfast love!

MAY 15, 2011

Fourth Sunday of Easter
Joanne Carlson Brown

COLOR
White

SCRIPTURE READINGS
Acts 2:42-47; Psalm 23; 1 Peter 2:19-25; John 10:1-10

THEME IDEAS
In general, we don't like being compared to sheep. And while the image of God as shepherd may be nostalgically comforting, it doesn't fit with our everyday lives. But focusing on a God who loves us deeply, who takes care of us and guides us along the way, who will never abandon us, and who calls us by name is an image worth lifting up and preserving, even if it is expressed in an anachronistic way.

INVITATION AND GATHERING

Call to Worship (Psalm 23, John 10)
Can you hear the voice of God?
We hear God calling us by name.
Are you troubled or distressed?
We come here to find a place to rest for awhile.
Come and find a guide who knows these lands.
We come to praise our Shepherding God,
whose pathways and doors lead to life.

Opening Prayer (Psalm 23, John 10)

Shepherding God,
   bring us into your fold.
Lead us beside still waters
   and restore our souls.
Help us see the way we should go,
   the way we should live.
Help us hear your voice calling our name.
Enliven this time of worship,
   that we may find true life
      as we join with others:
         praising your name,
            celebrating your great goodness,
               and sharing your love for all people.
Amen.

PROCLAMATION AND RESPONSE

Prayer of Confession (Psalm 23, John 10)

Shepherding God,
   be with us in our need.
Like sheep who have gone astray—
   we have not heeded your voice,
      calling us to follow the right paths,
      beckoning us to lie down and be restored;
   we have acted as if our salvation lies
      in busyness and control.
We do not want to be sheep—
   dependent on a shepherd for everything.
We want to do it alone—
   to maintain our independence.
Forgive us for rejecting your shepherding care
   and your love and guidance.
Forgive us for our need to do it by ourselves,
   to be separate from the flock.
Forgive us for doubting your presence
   in times of trouble.

Forgive us our despair
    in the face of seemingly unrelenting evil
      and death.
Lead us back to the path of life. Amen.

Words of Assurance (1 Peter 2, John 10)
    Jesus said, I have come that you may have life
      and have it abundantly.
    In so confessing, we have returned to the shepherd,
      the guardian of our souls who welcomes us
      with open arms and a glad heart.
    Know that the shepherd of our lives
      never abandons us, is always calling our name,
      and unfailingly loves and forgives us.

Response to the Word (Psalm 23, John 10)
    We have heard the voice of God calling our name,
    calling us to the path of life.
    **We give thanks for these refreshing words
    of love.**

THANKSGIVING AND COMMUNION

Offering Prayer (John 10)
    Generous, life-giving God,
      you sent Jesus that we might have life
      and have it abundantly.
    In response to this great gift,
      we now offer ourselves and our resources.
    May these gifts help us as a church to be your voice,
      calling all people to abundant life
        and to their true identities
        as your beloved. Amen.

SENDING FORTH

Benediction (Psalm 23, John 10)
    We have been refreshed and restored.
    We have been called and guided.

Let us go forth knowing who our true shepherd is,
    following his path, secure in the knowledge
    that goodness and mercy will follow us
    all the days of our life. Amen.

CONTEMPORARY OPTIONS

Gathering Words (John 10)

Hey, you sheep. Yes, you over there.
Can't you hear the shepherd calling—
    calling you to come and join with the others?
There's life and love and care and direction here
    just waiting for you to hear and see.
So come on in through the gate.
He's been waiting for you.

Praise Sentences (Psalm 23)

God is my shepherd!
God leads me all the way!
Goodness and mercy go with me all the time!
I've got a home with God forever!

MAY 22, 2011

Fifth Sunday of Easter
B. J. Beu

COLOR

White

SCRIPTURE READINGS

Acts 7:55-60; Psalm 31:1-5, 15-16; 1 Peter 2:2-10;
John 14:1-14

THEME IDEAS

Shelter, safety, and growth in Christ's spirit focus these
Easter readings. The psalmist seeks God's refuge and
strength against the snares of life. In John's Gospel, Jesus
offers assurances that even in death we will be with God,
for God's house has many dwelling places. The epistle
writer reminds us that we are spiritual infants who need
the nurture of pure, spiritual milk. If we are to grow like
Christ and become a royal priesthood, we must become
like Christ—we must become living stones of the house
of God. No one should be confused, however, that God
assures us a safe journey. Acts shows us the plight of
Stephen, who as a disciple of Jesus glimpsed the heavenly
kingdom but was not spared a violent death for his faith.
Ours is not a Pollyanna faith—a faith promising protection from harm—ours is a faith promising growth in the
Spirit in the midst of life's storms.

INVITATION AND GATHERING

Call to Worship (1 Peter 2)

Once we were not a people.
Now we are God's people.
Once we lived in darkness.
Now we dwell in marvelous light.
Let us drink from the pure, spiritual milk.
Let us grow into the salvation so freely offered.
Taste and see that the Lord is good.
We rejoice that God is always there.

Opening Prayer (Psalm 31, 1 Peter 2, John 14)

God of refuge and strength,
open our hearts to the words of your Son:
"Do not let your hearts be troubled.
Believe in God, believe also in me."
During this Easter season,
as we abide in the assurance of your care,
help us move beyond the comforting promise
of eternal life in your heavenly dwelling place
to embrace a deeper hunger and longing
to grow into a spiritual house
during our lives here on earth.
In the name of the master builder and the living stone,
the one who builds us into a spiritual house, amen.

PROCLAMATION AND RESPONSE

Prayer of Confession (Acts 7, 1 Peter 2, John 14)

Living God,
we love to hear Jesus' assurance
that he has prepared a place for us
in your heavenly kingdom,
but we fear the challenge to live our faith
if it means, like Stephen before us,
that we might suffer for our beliefs;

we rejoice in the knowledge
that we may entrust our spirit to you
in certain hope of eternal life,
but we shudder at your call
to drink of your spiritual milk
if it means that we must really change
as we grow into salvation.
Give us the courage of Stephen
and the confidence of Peter,
that we may be a holy priesthood—
a people built like living stones
into a spiritual house. Amen.

Words of Assurance (John 14:1, 13-14)
Jesus said: "Do not let your hearts be troubled.
Believe in God, believe also in me....
I will do whatever you ask in my name,
so that the Father may be glorified in the Son.
If in my name you ask me for anything,
I will do it."

Response to the Word (1 Peter 2, John 14)
Come to Christ, the living stone. And like living stones,
allow God to build you into a spiritual house. For in that
house you will come to know that God dwells within you,
and you abide in God. Thanks be to God!

THANKSGIVING AND COMMUNION

Offering Prayer (Psalm 31, 1 Peter 2)
God of overflowing abundance,
you have fed us on your spiritual milk
and nourished us on your heavenly food.
When the snares of this world
threatened to overwhelm us,
you have been our fortress and our rock,
saving us from the net that is hidden from us.
As people thankful for the mercy we have received,

we entrust our lives and our spirit into your care,
offering you our gifts,
in the hope that they may reflect your light
for all to see. Amen.

SENDING FORTH

Benediction (1 Peter 2, John 14)
Once we were not a people.
Now we are God's people.
Once we lived in darkness.
Now we dwell in marvelous light.
Once our souls wanted for nourishment.
**Now we have been fed
on God's pure, spiritual milk.**
Once our hearts were troubled.
Now we rest secure.

CONTEMPORARY OPTIONS

Gathering Words (1 Peter 2, John 14)
What's that stone there, the one cast aside?
That's the stone the builders rejected.
Isn't it any good?
**Are you kidding? It's the cornerstone
of God's house!**
It looks alive.
It is, and through God, we too are living stones.
Can you build anything with living stones?
God can, if we're willing.
If we're willing?
**God can build us into a spiritual house—
if we're willing.**
Thanks be to God!

Praise Sentences (1 Peter 2)
Christ is our living rock!
Worship the cornerstone of our faith.
Christ is our living rock!

MAY 29, 2011

Sixth Sunday of Easter
Rebecca J. Kruger Gaudino

COLOR
White

SCRIPTURE READINGS
Acts 17:22-31; Psalm 66:8-20; 1 Peter 3:13-22; John 14:15-21

THEME IDEAS

In Acts, Paul describes God as the source of all creation and the source of life for all humankind. More than this, "we live and move and have our being" *in* God. Indeed, how can this God be far from us when we are *in* God? First Peter speaks of our being brought *to* God by Jesus Christ and describes lives of integrity "*in* Christ." John takes this human/divine spatial imagery the furthest in Jesus' description of himself as *in* God, while we the disciples are *in* Christ and Christ is *in* us. More than this, the Spirit is *with* us and *in* us as well. These passages call us to recognize the mysterious interrelationship that undergirds our being; they challenge us to live lives of love and goodness, courage and hope.

INVITATION AND GATHERING

Call to Worship *(Acts 17, Psalm 66)*
(This liturgy may be done with any combination of one to four leaders.)

Leader 1:   Come and hear, all you who fear God, and we will tell what God has done for us.

Leader 2:   God is the Sovereign of heaven and earth, maker of this world and all within it.

Leader 3:   God has given to all mortals life and breath and every blessing.

Leader 4:   Bless our God, O peoples!
Let the sound of God's praise be heard.

People: **Blessed be God! Blessed be God! Blessed be God!**

Opening Prayer *(Acts 17, Psalm 66, John 14)*
Source of all creation, maker of the world
    and everything in it,
    you are never far from each one of us.
We come into your house seeking you,
    O giver of life and breath.
Reveal yourself to us; dwell with us;
    and abide in us.
We live because of you.
We hope because of you.
In the name of Jesus Christ in whom we live,
    and the Spirit of Truth who abides in us, amen.

PROCLAMATION AND RESPONSE

Prayer of Confession *(Acts 17, John 14)*
Maker and giver of all,
    forgive us when we are too preoccupied
        to notice your presence in our lives:
    when we walk through this world
        and fail to see the wonder
            of you upholding our lives and all creation;

when we walk through our lives
and fail to see you abiding with, within,
and around us;
when we walk through holy moments
and fail to savor your presence,
instead feeling abandoned
in the vast sweep of life
as each day rushes at us
with its demands.
Open our eyes to your presence, God of love,
that we may lean on you—
for you uphold all of creation
in tenderness and power. Amen.

Words of Assurance (Acts 17, Psalm 66, John 14)
When Jesus left the disciples, he gave us a promise:
"I will not leave you orphaned!"
For we, his disciples, live in him and he in us—
the presence of God within and around all.
What a promise! Take courage! Take comfort!
Blessed be God!

Passing the Peace of Christ (Acts 17, John 14)
Because Jesus Christ is in us, and we in him, his peace is
a powerful gift that we may share with others. Pass the
blessing of this peace to your brothers and sisters in Christ
and to all the children of God.

Response to the Word (Acts 17, John 14, 1 Peter 3)
O God,
in you we live and move and have our being!
May we live out this profound truth,
mindful of the beauty, the hope, and the calling
of living in you. Amen.

THANKSGIVING AND COMMUNION

Invitation to the Offering (Acts 17, 1 Peter 3)
We are invited to give an accounting of the hope that sustains us, the love and presence of God that upholds all.

Out of this sustaining hope, let us give our gifts today for those who also need this hope.

Offering Prayer (Acts 17, 1 Peter 3, John 14)
>Giver of all gifts,
>>we are grateful for your every blessing
>>>and for your presence through all of life—
>>>>in our joys and fears,
>>>>and in our hopes and dreads.
>We pray for those who do not know
>>the consolation of your presence in their lives,
>>>asking that you reveal yourself to them
>>>>through the gifts we have given
>>>>and through the lives we live.
>Reveal yourself, O God,
>>that all your children
>>>may find their true home in you. Amen.

SENDING FORTH

Benediction (Acts 17, 1 Peter 3, John 14)
>Wherever we are, we are in God.
>>**Wherever we are, we are in Christ,**
>>**and Christ is in us.**
>Wherever we are, the Spirit abides with us and in us.
>>**We go forth in peace and hope,**
>>**upheld by God in every way.**
>Let us go forth in faithfulness and trust.
>>**May all see the Divine in and through us.**

CONTEMPORARY OPTIONS

Gathering Words (Acts 17, Psalm 66, John 15)
>Come into God's house!
>Come and hear what God has done!
>>**God has made the world**
>>**and breathed the breath of life into us!**
>But God hasn't stopped there. There's more!
>God is still on the scene, upholding all our life,

surrounding us in power and love.
We live, move, and have our very being in God!
Let the sound of God's praise be heard!
Praise God! Praise God! Praise God!

Praise Sentences

Blessed is the maker of the world,
     giver of life and breath!
In you, O God, we live and move
     and have our being!

JUNE 5, 2011

Ascension Sunday
Leigh Anne Taylor

COLOR
White

SCRIPTURE READINGS
Acts 1:1-11; Psalm 47; Ephesians 1:15-23; Luke 24:44-53

THEME IDEAS
Christians confess that Jesus fulfilled the promises of God as written in the Law, the Prophets, and the Psalms. God raised Jesus Christ from the dead, and Jesus Christ ascended to God where he has ultimate authority with God. From this place of authority, Jesus Christ is the head of the church, whose purpose is to proclaim repentance and forgiveness of sins to the entire earth by the power of the Holy Spirit. In today's readings, Jesus blesses his followers, telling them to proclaim repentance and forgiveness in his name. But first they must wait in Jerusalem for the coming of the Holy Spirit. His followers return to the temple to worship God where one can imagine that they sang Psalm 47, which celebrates God's ultimate authority over all.

INVITATION AND GATHERING

Call to Worship (Psalm 47)

Clap your hands, all you people!
Shout to God with loud songs of joy!
Sing praises to God, sing praises!
Sing praises to our sovereign Lord!
God is sovereign over all the earth!
Sing praises to God, sing praises!
Let everything that has breath sing praises.
Shout to God with loud songs of joy!

Opening Prayer (Ephesians 1, Acts 1)

God of all glory,
as we come to know your Son
through the living word of scripture,
enlighten our hearts
with the spirit of wisdom and revelation.
Remind us again of Christ's authority over the church
at all times and in all places.
Renew in us again our purpose as Christ's followers:
to proclaim repentance and forgiveness of sins
in the name of Jesus Christ
to all people in all places.
All glory and honor be to you, Christ Jesus. Amen.

PROCLAMATION AND RESPONSE

Prayer of Confession (Psalm 47, Ephesians 1)

Our Savior Jesus,
even while we extol you as Divine Sovereign
whose authority is above all earthly power,
we have failed to give you authority
over even the smallest matters of our lives.
We confess our arrogant,
self-centered exercise of power
over matters in our lives (*pause*),
in our church (*pause*),
and in our world. (*pause*)

We desperately cling to our own power,
    failing to yield to your divine authority,
      wisdom, guidance, and love.
Forgive us, we pray,
    for the harm we have done to others
      and to ourselves.
In your mercy, save us, Lord. Amen.

Words of Assurance (Luke 24)

Jesus said to his disciples before he ascended to God,
    "Repentance and forgiveness of sins is to be proclaimed
    in my name to all nations."
Repent then, followers of Christ,
    and allow Christ to transform your lives.
Receive forgiveness in the name of the risen savior. Amen.

Passing the Peace of Christ (Ephesians 1)

Paul writes to the Christian community at Ephesus, "I have heard of your faith in the Lord Jesus and your love toward all the saints, and for this reason I do not cease to give thanks for you as I remember you in my prayers." Near you now are people whose courageous expressions and acts of selfless love have profoundly influenced your lives. With thankfulness, let us greet one another in the name of the risen Christ.

Response to the Word (Ephesians 1)

Holy Lord,
    the gift of your hope and the power of your Spirit
      are given to all who believe,
      even to us who worship here today.
Help us grasp the enormity of your gifts,
    that we may receive these gifts with open hearts
      and celebrate them joyfully
        as we serve you in every aspect of our lives. Amen.

THANKSGIVING AND COMMUNION

Invitation to the Offering (Acts 1)

If Jesus was giving directions to his disciples today, they might sound something like this: "You will be my witnesses to *(your home town)*, to all of *(your county)*, to *(your state)*, and to the ends of the earth."

One way we become Christ's witnesses is through our giving today. Some of our gifts will help people in Jesus' name locally through *(mention a local ministry)*. Some funds will reach into our state through *(mention a conference or regional ministry)*. Some gifts will reach far into our world in the name of Jesus through our support of *(mention an international ministry that you support)*. I invite you to give generously and joyfully as you fulfill Christ's call to be his witnesses to *(your town, your county, your state)*, and to all the world.

Offering Prayer
We thank you, O God,
   for your many gifts,
      which make us what we are.
Receive these gifts that we bring today
   in token and thanks,
      for the love we have received
         from your gracious hand. Amen.
(B. J. Beu)

SENDING FORTH

Benediction (Acts 1)
People of God, receive the blessing of Jesus Christ
   and the power of the Holy Spirit.
Go now to live in Christian love
   and witness to the power of forgiveness
   in your homes, in your community,
   even to the ends of the earth,
   until that day when Christ returns in glory. Amen.

CONTEMPORARY OPTIONS

Gathering Words (Psalm 47)
Everybody here, clap your hands!
God is in the house!

Everybody here, shout your praise to God!
God is in the house!
Everybody here, sing praise to God!
God is in the house!

Praise Sentences (Psalm 47, Ephesians 1)
Jesus Christ is the Ruler of all rulers.
Exalt the name of Jesus!
Jesus Christ is the Lord of all lords.
Exalt the name of Jesus!
Jesus Christ is the Name above all names.
Exalt the name of Jesus!

JUNE 12, 2011

Pentecost Sunday
Matthew J. Packer

COLOR
Red

SCRIPTURE READINGS
Acts 2:1-21; Psalm 104:24-34, 35b; 1 Corinthians 12:3b-13;
John 7:37-39

THEME IDEAS
Today's scripture passages highlight the multifaceted nature of the Holy Spirit. The Spirit ushers in the Day of the
Lord (Acts 2:17-20). The Spirit brings about new life
(Psalm 104:30). The Spirit offers a variety of gifts
(1 Corinthians 12:4). Finally, the Spirit proceeds from Jesus
(John 7:38). Human response to the activity of the Spirit
is bewildering (Acts 2:6), raises questions (Acts 2:12), and
invites derision (Acts 2:13). When the gifts of the Spirit are
approached with awe and gratitude, however, we experience transformational grace.

INVITATION AND GATHERING

Call to Worship (Acts 2, 1 Corinthians 12, John 7)
The Spirit comes as a violent wind,
filling this place of worship.

The Spirit comes as tongues of fire,
resting on those who are gathered here.
The Spirit comes, and we are transformed.
Jew and Greek, slave and free,
all are welcome to drink of one Spirit.
Come, Holy Spirit,
fill us; fill this place; inhabit our lives;
bless our worship.

Opening Prayer (Psalm 104:24, 30)

Life-giving Lord,
we offer praise with all of creation
for the wonders and works that surround us
every moment of our lives.
Send forth your Spirit,
that we may be recreated and renewed,
to love and live for you.
In the matchless name of your Son, Jesus Christ,
we pray. Amen.

PROCLAMATION AND RESPONSE

Prayer of Confession (Acts 2, John 7)

(The unison words are lines 1-4 of the hymn "Spirit of the Liv-
ing God," and may be sung or spoken. If the unison words are
spoken rather than sung, consider changing "me" to "you" to
elicit reflection on these familiar phrases.)
Spirit of the living God, fall afresh on me.
Gracious God, Source of the Spirit,
forgive us for doubting your goodness
when you work in ways we do not understand.
Spirit of the living God, fall afresh on me.
Loving Christ, Wellspring of the Spirit,
forgive us for failing to follow your example
of compassion and service.
Melt me, mold me, fill me, use me.
Holy Spirit, Living Water,
forgive us for misusing your gifts

when we focus more on ourselves than on others.
Spirit of the living God, fall afresh on me.

Words of Assurance (Acts 2, Psalm 104:30)

God declares, "I will pour out my Spirit upon all flesh . . .
and everyone who calls on the name of the Lord
shall be saved."
Know with confidence that, by God's grace,
you are forgiven and renewed.

Passing the Peace of Christ

As a forgiven and renewed people, share the peace of
Christ with those around you.

Response to the Word (Psalm 104)

Lord God,
we have heard your living word:
may our meditation be pleasing to you;
may our hearts and minds be transformed;
and may a new song be sung in our souls.
Amen and amen.

THANKSGIVING AND COMMUNION

Invitation to the Offering (Psalm 104:28)

The psalmist tells us that God provides for all living
things: "When you give to them, they gather it up; /
when you open your hand, they are filled with good
things." God has graciously given to us. In gratitude and
joy, let us offer back to God the bounty by which we have
been blessed.

Offering Prayer (Psalm 104, John 7)

Gift-giving God,
thank you for filling us with good things.
Life-giving Spirit,
thank you for blessing our lives
and drawing us ever deeper
into fellowship with Christ.

May the offerings we present today
bless those who thirst for the living water
that only you can provide.
In your holy name we pray. Amen.

SENDING FORTH

Benediction (1 Corinthians 12:12)
May the Spirit of the living God
continue to fall afresh on you
as you go from this place.
Though we are now divided,
remember that we are always one
in Christ Jesus.
Go and share unity in the Spirit
as you live lives of wholeness and peace.

CONTEMPORARY OPTIONS

Gathering Words (Psalm 104)
The glory of the Lord endures forever.
Rejoice in God's holy works.
Sing to the Lord as long as you live.
I will sing praise to my God while I draw breath.
Bless the Lord, O my soul.
Praise the Lord!

Praise Sentences (1 Corinthians 12)
Praise the Spirit who makes us one body!
**For in the one Spirit we were all baptized
into one body.**
Praise God who binds us all together.
**Jews or Greeks, slave or free,
we are all one body in Christ!**
Praise God!
Praise God!

JUNE 19, 2011

Trinity Sunday
Father's Day
Mary J. Scifres

COLOR
White

SCRIPTURE READINGS
Genesis 1:1–2:4a; Psalm 8; 2 Corinthians 13:11-13;
Matthew 28:16-20

THEME IDEAS
Trinity Sunday scriptures always puzzle me. Should we
focus on the Trinity, or on discipleship and evangelism?
For today's theme, I invite you to focus on the goodness
of creation, with particular emphasis on God's call for the
human creation to be a special blessing for the world.
Whether we are blessing the earth with conservation and
simplicity, blessing the earth's creatures with care and
compassion, or blessing humans by sharing the good
news of Christ's teachings, we are answering that call first
given at creation: to be fruitful and to care responsibly for
this earth. What a blessed way to live in God's image!

INVITATION AND GATHERING

Call to Worship (Genesis 1, Psalm 8)
Look at the heavens, God's glorious works,
and know that God has made us more glorious still!

God created us, godly and good.
Rejoice in this blessing: God is mindful of us.
God created us in the very likeness of God!
Take heed of our call to be caretakers and stewards.
God created us to be a blessing for all.

Opening Prayer (Genesis 1)

Creator God,
   we thank and praise you
      for the many gifts of your creation:
         for sun and moon, water and sky,
            stars in the heavens
               and creatures on the earth;
   we thank and praise you
      for entrusting us to be your special creation:
         made in your image, given responsibility
            for this magnificent earth.
As we worship this day,
   open our hearts and minds
      to see ourselves as caretakers
         and stewards of this earth.
Help us see where we may walk more gently
   and live more compassionately,
      that all of your earth might find in us
         your very image, nurturing and caring
            in all that we do.

PROCLAMATION AND RESPONSE

Prayer of Confession (Genesis 1, Psalm 8)

God of grace and glory,
   forgive us when we do not glorify you
      in our actions upon this earth.
When we rule as if we were dictators and oppressors,
   forgive our selfish ways.
When we take from the earth and its creatures
   as if they were our servants and slaves,
      forgive our selfish ways.

When we forget that you have called us
  to be your image of creative nurture,
  forgive our negligence and ignorance.
Create in us clean hearts,
  that we may be made more truly in your image.
In the name of God the Creator,
  the Redeemer, and the Sustainer, we pray. Amen.

Words of Assurance (Psalm 8)
What are we that God is mindful of us?
Even stars millions of miles away
  seem to shine more brightly.
And yet, God is mindful of us.
God has crowned us with glory and honor.
In Christ, God has renewed this promise
  and offered forgiveness and grace,
  that we may be born anew and created afresh
  through the power of the Holy Spirit.
Receive Christ's forgiveness.
Receive new birth in the Spirit.
Receive God's creative love! Amen.

Passing the Peace of Christ (2 Corinthians 13)
Sisters and brothers, be at peace with one another and
with God, for God's peace is ours even now. Share this
peace as we greet one another with a holy kiss and other
signs of peace and love.

Response to the Word (Genesis 1, Psalm 8, Matthew 28)
In the beginning, God created the heavens
and the earth.
  And God called this creation good.
In the beginning, God said, "Let there be light."
  And God called this creation good.
In the beginning, God separated water from sky,
and earth from sea.
  And God called this creation good.

In the beginning, God brought forth plants and trees,
the sun and the moon, and the stars up in the sky.
And God called this creation good.
In the beginning, God brought forth creatures
and beasts, birds and fish, living upon the earth.
And God called this creation good.
In the beginning, God created humankind,
in God's very image, crowning us
with blessing and glory.
And God called this creation good.
To the end of the age, God creates us still,
calling us to bless this beloved earth.
May we love so that God calls this creation good.

THANKSGIVING AND COMMUNION

Invitation to the Offering (Genesis 1, Matthew 28)
God has given us this amazing earth. God has given us
this amazing life. Let us show our gratitude by returning
a portion of God's gifts to the church and to its work in
the world.

Offering Prayer (Genesis 1)
Creator God,
    your gifts overwhelm us.
We thank you for sharing this amazing creation
    with us.
We praise you for the glory of being created
    in your very image.
We pray that these gifts
    may reflect the glory of your image
        and go forth to truly bless
            your creation upon this earth.

SENDING FORTH

Benediction (2 Corinthians 13)
May the grace of Christ Jesus
    flow over and through you.

May the love of God live in and around you.
May the communion of the Holy Spirit
  be with each and every one of you.
May we all go forth as God's blessed creation,
  God's image of love and grace.

—Or—

Benediction (Matthew 28)
Go into all the world as bearers of God's good news.
Teach and be taught as disciples of Jesus Christ.
Baptize and bless as children of the Holy Spirit.
And may the grace of Christ, the creative love of God,
  and the power of the Holy Spirit go with you all.

CONTEMPORARY OPTIONS

Gathering Words (Genesis 1, Matthew 28)
Come, sisters and brothers,
we are God's own children.
  God proclaims us blessed and good.
Shine, brothers and sisters,
we are made in the image of God.
  God proclaims us blessed and good.
Live, sisters and brothers,
we are created to be caregivers of creation.
  God proclaims us blessed and good.
Trust, sisters and brothers,
we are God's beloved.
  **Praise be to God who blesses us
  and calls us good.**

Praise Sentences (Psalm 8)
O Lord, our God, how majestic is your name
in all the earth!
  Your glory is all around!
O Lord, our God, how majestic is your name
in all the earth!
  Your glory is all around!

JUNE 26, 2011

Second Sunday after Pentecost
B. J. Beu

COLOR
Green

SCRIPTURE READINGS
Genesis 22:1-14; Psalm 13; Romans 6:12-23;
Matthew 10:40-42

THEME IDEAS
No matter how hard we try, we cannot avoid the pain and
trials of life. The psalmist speaks of the trials of faith, as we
seek God's comfort and protection. Genesis highlights the
trials of conflicting loyalties, as we struggle to follow God
while living with personal integrity and loyalty to those
we love. Romans illustrates the trials of earthly passions
and sinful temptations, even as we aspire to walk with
Christ. Yet, in the midst of our pain and fears of aban-
donment, God is there to rescue us and lead us safely
home.

INVITATION AND GATHERING

Call to Worship (Genesis 22, Psalm 13)
You seem far away, O Lord.
Our faith is sorely tested.

Do not hide your face from us forever.
We put our trust in your steadfast love.
How long must our souls bear this pain?
How much more can we lose before we break?
Yet we place our trust in your goodness and mercy.
Our hearts will rejoice in your salvation.

Opening Prayer (Psalm 13, Matthew 10)
God of pain and suffering,
   you embrace us in our need.
As we enter this house of worship,
   you know our deepest need;
   you embrace our most desperate hopes.
Come to us and quicken the spirit
   that languishes within us.
Live in us this day,
   that we may be a people
     who rise above the storms
      that threaten to overcome us.
We ask this through the one who came
   that we might have life
   and have it abundantly. Amen.

PROCLAMATION AND RESPONSE

Prayer of Confession (Genesis 22, Psalm 13)
Merciful God,
   as we travel the difficult paths of life,
   and our way forward is challenged
     at every turn,
     it is easy to forget
      that you are always there.
We feel alone,
   abandoned to our fate.
Forgive our preoccupation,
   when we cry out in anguish:
     "What have I done to deserve this?"

Overlook our self-absorption,
  when we forget that you seek our salvation,
    not our pain.
For your ways lead to life, O God,
  not to death.
Teach us to feel your presence,
  even in the midst of our deepest despair,
    that we may rise above our fear and doubt
      and embrace your grace and mercy. Amen.

Assurance of Pardon (Romans 6:23)
Hear the word of God: "The wages of sin is death,
  but the free gift of God is eternal life
  in Christ Jesus our Lord."

Prayer of Lament or
Reflection on the Word (Genesis 22)
God of a thousand names,
  God with a thousand faces,
    your ways are hidden from us.
We read that you asked Abraham
  to sacrifice his beloved son, Isaac.
In horror, we watch the event unfold
  in our minds' eye:
    Isaac wondering why his father
      has brought no animal for the sacrifice;
    Isaac realizing that the God his father loves
      is more important to him
        than the life of his own son;
    Isaac watching his father raise the knife
      to spill his blood on the altar.
We read that this was only a test—
  a test of faith.
We hear that Abraham passed the test—
  that he was found worthy
    to be the father of your people.
But we wonder, God,
  did Abraham really pass the test?

If Abraham was found faithful,
- why do the Hebrew people
   bear the name of Jacob,
   who wrestled with you all night
   and earned the name Israel
   through the struggle?
Why do your people not bear the name of Abraham,
   who put up no struggle,
   but simply submitted
   when asked to kill his son?
We wonder, O God, we wonder.
Did you really ask such a thing of Abraham,
   even as a test of faith?
We confess, O God, that if this is faith,
   we are not up to it.
Your ways remain hidden, O God,
   your holiness shrouded in mystery.

THANKSGIVING AND COMMUNION

Offering Prayer (Genesis 22)

Bountiful God,
   when we come to you with nothing,
      you yourself provide the offering;
   when the burden of our sacrifice
      threatens to overwhelm us,
      you spare us the deadly cost.
In tribute and thanks
   for your manifold blessings,
   we offer you what we have
      in certain hope
         of your abiding love. Amen.

SENDING FORTH

Benediction (Genesis 22, Romans 6)

The One who cut Isaac free from the ropes
that bound him releases us from our bondage
to sin and death.

We go forth as those sanctified with eternal life
with hearts lightened by your joy.
The One who freed us from our bondage
sends us to heal a world enslaved by fear and doubt.
**We go forth to loose the cords of the bound
and heal the wounds of the afflicted.**
Thanks be to God.

CONTEMPORARY OPTIONS

Gathering Words (Matthew 10)
In Christ Jesus you are welcome here.
In Christ Jesus all are welcome here.
Welcome, prophets and little children,
in Christ's name.
Welcome, people of God!

Praise Sentences (Psalm 13)
Even when you are afraid, sing to the Lord.
Sing to the Lord.
Even when God seems far away,
rejoice in your salvation.
Rejoice in God's salvation.
Sing to the Lord.
Sing to the Lord.
Sing to the Lord.

JULY 3, 2011

Third Sunday after Pentecost

Mary J. Scifres

COLOR

Green

SCRIPTURE READINGS

Genesis 24:34-38, 42-49, 58-67; Psalm 45:10-17;
Romans 7:15-25a; Matthew 11:16-19, 25-30

THEME IDEAS

For the next five weeks, the Hebrew scriptures recount the
stories of Isaac and Rebekah and their children. Although
the lessons during the Ordinary season are not chosen to
interrelate to one another, themes often emerge that allow
us to integrate the scriptures or utilize worship words
from scriptures different than the one that may inspire the
week's sermon. Today, the yoke of following is seen in a
variety of settings. Abraham's servant travels far from
home to find a wife for Isaac. Rebekah, with the blessing
of her family, travels far from her home to marry Isaac.
Paul delights in God's law, even as he struggles to live the
righteous life demanded by that law. Jesus calls us to take
on the yoke of God's love, promising a light burden, even
as he laments his rejection by the very people he is called
to save. All of these yokes bring joy that lighten our load,
for we are following God. But these yokes also bring
the burden of rejection, of unfamiliar journeys, and of

frustration as we seek, with mixed results, to follow faithfully at every step. Take heart! Forgiveness is ours through God's gentle and gracious heart.

INVITATION AND GATHERING

Call to Worship (Matthew 11)
Christ calls: "Come to me, all who are weary
and burdened."
In Christ, we find rest.
Christ calls, "Bear my yoke and learn from me."
In Christ, we see God's ways.
Christ promises, "I am gentle and humble in heart."
In Christ, we know God's love.
Christ proclaims, "My yoke is easy,
and my burden is light."
In Christ, we find strength.
Come, you who are weary or burdened,
joy-filled or sorrowful. Christ has called us here.

Opening Prayer (Matthew 11)
(This prayer may lead into the hymn "Lift Every Voice and Sing.")
God of our weary years,
　　you have walked with us
　　　　through the many miles of our travels.
God of our silent tears,
　　you have comforted and strengthened us
　　　　for this journey.
Even as you have led us into the light of your ways,
　　keep us on your path,
　　　　now and forevermore.
When the way is easy and the burden is gentle,
　　help us turn to you for guidance and strength.
As we lift our voices in song,
　　may we also lift our lives
　　　　in the cause of justice and righteousness,
　　　　learning and living your ways
　　　　　　each and every day.

PROCLAMATION AND RESPONSE

Prayer of Confession (Romans 7, Matthew 11)
> Merciful God,
>> we do not understand our own actions—
>>> we do not do the things we want,
>>>> yet we do the very things we detest.
>> Forgive our foolish ways.
>> Reclaim us as children of your promise.
>> Give us the strength and the courage
>>> to bear your yoke willingly
>>>> and heed your call faithfully.
>> In Christ's name, we pray. Amen.

Words of Assurance (Romans 7, Matthew 11)
> Who will rescue us from our foolish ways
>> and misguided acts?
> Only Christ, who is gentle and humble of heart.
> In Christ, God's yoke is made easier,
>> God's burden lighter.
> For in Christ, we are made perfect,
>> even in our imperfection.
> Thanks be to God!

Passing the Peace of Christ (Matthew 11)
> As Christ has offered us God's gentle and humble heart, may we turn with gentle and humble hearts to one another and offer words and signs of love and peace.

Response to the Word (Genesis 24, Romans 7, Matthew 11)
> Abraham and Sarah heard God's call,
>> **and Sarah and Abraham traveled**
>> **where God led.**
> Isaac and Rebekah heard God's call,
>> **and Rebekah traveled to Isaac as God led.**
> The God of our ancestors calls to us even now,
>> **and we will travel where God leads.**
> Thanks be to God through Jesus Christ,
> who strengthens us for the journey!

THANKSGIVING AND COMMUNION

Invitation to the Offering (Genesis 24, Matthew 11)
As Isaac offered gifts to show his commitment to Rebekah,
so now we offer our gifts as signs of our commitment to
God. May we give of ourselves, that others will see in us
persons who dance when Christ celebrates and who
mourn when Christ wails for the needs of God's world.

Offering Prayer (Psalm 45)
Generous God,
may the gifts we return to you
cause your name to be celebrated
among the nations.
May the lives that we live
cause your name to be celebrated
in all generations.
May our offerings be signs of our praise to you,
forever and ever. Amen.

Call to Communion (Matthew 11:28)
"Come to me, all you that are weary and are carrying
heavy burdens, and I will give you rest." Christ calls to us
now and invites to the table all who yearn for the gentle
and loving heart of God. Come, for Christ's yoke is easy
and God's burden is light. Come, all are welcome here.

SENDING FORTH

Benediction (Genesis 24, Romans 7, Matthew 11)
Go forth with the confidence of Rebekah,
who left all behind to follow God.
Go forth with the delight of Paul,
who knew that in Christ we are set free to follow!
Go forth with the grace of Jesus Christ,
who carries us as we bear the yoke of following.
Go forth, dancing with praise for God
and living with Christ's love for the world!

CONTEMPORARY OPTIONS

Gathering Words

Are we a generation of complainers, cynics,
and critics?
  Rescue us for lives of joyful following!
Are we a people who refuse to dance
when Christ plays?
  Rescue us for lives of joyful following!
Are we a people hardened by the world's woes
who neglect to mourn for those in despair?
  Rescue us for lives of joyful following!
Are we a people afraid to follow where God leads?
  Rescue us for lives of joyful following!
Christ *has* rescued us from negative thoughts,
freeing us for lives of joyful following.
  **Thanks be to God! Let us praise Jesus Christ
  and answer God's call!**

Praise Sentences (Psalm 45)

Let's celebrate God's love every day!
  Praise God forever and ever!
Let's celebrate God's love every day!
  Praise God forever and ever!

JULY 10, 2011

Fourth Sunday after Pentecost
Mary J. Scifres

COLOR

Green

SCRIPTURE READINGS

Genesis 25:19-34; Psalm 119:105-12; Romans 8:1-11;
Matthew 13:1-9, 18-23

THEME IDEAS

Rebekah's children struggle within her. Two parents
struggle to love their children equally; yet each clearly has
a favorite. Two brothers struggle to find their place in
God's world as they answer God's call. Christians struggle to live in the Spirit rather than in the flesh. Seeds struggle to take root and grow. The struggle of living and
growing as children of God's Spirit is a struggle that has
haunted humanity since the dawn of time. Today's scriptures reflect those struggles, even as they offer words that
can become lamps to our feet and light for our journey of
growth in the Spirit.

INVITATION AND GATHERING

Call to Worship (Matthew 13)
God's word is being sown in our very lives.
Listen, my heart, to God's word this day.

Christ's teachings are being scattered and sown
in this very room.
  Open, my soul, and receive the seeds
  of Christ's wisdom.
The Spirit is here to nourish and strengthen us.
  Grow, my spirit, and be fertile ground
  for a life bearing the fruit of Christ's love
  in all that I say and in all that I do. Amen.

Opening Prayer (Genesis 25, Psalm 119, Matthew 13)

God of growth and new beginnings,
    enter into the struggles of our lives.
Nurture our souls,
      that we may be fertile ground
        for wisdom and love
          to spring forth in our lives.
Dwell within us,
      that we may have strength of purpose
        to live out your calling
          each and every day.
Let the words of your scriptures
      and the teaching of your Son Jesus
        be a light to our path
          and a lamp to our feet.
In Jesus' name, we pray. Amen.

PROCLAMATION AND RESPONSE

Prayer of Confession (Genesis 25, Romans 8, Matthew 13)

Strong and strengthening God,
      forgive us when we trust our own strength
        and follow our own wily ways;
      forgive us when we are rocky or barren followers,
        who listen but do not fully receive your word;
      forgive us when we are too tentative or troubled
        to allow your word to bloom
          fully and abundantly in our lives.

Strengthen us to rest in your promise
and to live in your Spirit,
that as you plant your word upon our hearts,
it may take root and grow.
Nurture us with your grace and mercy,
that we may not be empty, barren vessels,
but fruitful followers of Christ
and life-giving children of your Spirit.
In Christ's name, we pray. Amen.

Words of Assurance (Romans 8, Matthew 13)
All who are in the Spirit of God have been set free.
And those who are in Christ Jesus
are free from condemnation.
As forgiven people made new in God's Spirit,
be fertile ground for God's word
to take root and grow.
Thanks be to God!

Passing the Peace of Christ (Romans 8)
Setting our minds on the Spirit, the giver of life and peace,
let us share God's peace with one another.

Preparing to Hear the Word or Benediction (Psalm 119)
God's word is a lamp to our feet.
Christ's teachings are a light to our path.
The decrees of God are our heritage forever.
These teachings bring us joy.
May these words be planted in our souls
and take root in our lives, today and every day.

THANKSGIVING AND COMMUNION

Invitation to the Offering (Genesis 25, Matthew 13)
We are both sower and seed, struggling children and nurturing parents. May we offer ourselves to God's work,
planting and sowing, blooming and growing, struggling
and learning, caring and nurturing. May we give of our-

selves generously, that God's love may bear abundant fruit in our lives.

Offering Prayer (Matthew 13)
God of all creation,
create through us your realm upon this earth.
With these offerings,
help us plant seeds
even as we bear fruit.
Bless our efforts and nourish our lives,
that we may be a harvest
of generosity and love. Amen.

SENDING FORTH

Benediction (Romans 8, Matthew 13)
Plant in your hearts the words of this day.
May God's word take root in our lives.
Set in your minds the things of the Spirit.
May God's Spirit nourish our very souls.
Claim for your lives Christ's grace and guidance.
**May Christ's love bear fruit in our doing
and in our being, today and every day.**

CONTEMPORARY OPTIONS

Gathering Words (Psalm 119)
God's word is a lamp to our feet.
Christ's love is a light to our path.
God's word is a lamp to our feet.
Christ's love is a light to our path.

Praise Sentences (Romans 8)
The Spirit of God is with us now.
Praise God for Christ's abundant love!
The Spirit of God is with us now.
Praise God for Christ's abundant love!

JULY 17, 2011

Fifth Sunday after Pentecost
Mary J. Scifres

COLOR

Green

SCRIPTURE READINGS

Genesis 28:10-19a; Psalm 139:1-12, 23-24;
Romans 8:12-25; Matthew 13:24-30, 36-43

THEME IDEAS

Waiting for God's creative presence is never easy, and
sometimes God's presence is most unexpected. And yet,
inevitably, God arrives. God is with us. God is creating
and re-creating. Still, we struggle and groan alongside
God in this process. Jacob dreams of angels and recog-
nizes that God has been present with him; years later, his
nighttime encounter with God's angel will become a
wrestling match that leaves him permanently injured.
God's whole creation groans with the pangs of birthing
the hope of God's promises, and God's children strive to
grow alongside the weeds sown by enemies. Waiting for
God's creative presence is never easy. And yet, God arrives. God is with us. With God, we are creating and being
created even as we wait.

INVITATION AND GATHERING

Call to Worship (Genesis 28, Psalm 139)
God searches us and knows us,
calling us out of the darkness.
We enter God's house,
yearning to see God's presence
and walk in Christ's light.
God hems us in, behind and before,
with knowledge too wonderful for words.
We come now to worship,
yearning to know and to be known.
Come, enter God's house, the gate of heaven.
How awesome is God,
who comes to us now!

Opening Prayer (Genesis 28, Psalm 139)
O Lord,
you have searched us and known us
for all of our lives.
We thank you for your constant presence.
Still, we come to you now,
asking that you light our way
and guide our paths.
Descend to us and bless us
with knowledge of your presence.
Raise our thoughts to heavenly heights
and grant us your wisdom and your grace.
Hold us fast in this time of worship,
that we may feel your comfort
and discern your guidance.

PROCLAMATION AND RESPONSE

Prayer of Confession (Genesis 28, Psalm 139)
Eternal God,
you have searched us and known us.

You know when we fall short
  and when we rise to your calling.
You discern our thoughts,
  whether they be good or ill.
Hem us in, O God.
Remind us that we cannot hide from you,
  and we need not try.
Forgive us and love us into righteousness.
Lay your hand upon us,
    that we may love you and your creation
      more perfectly each day.
Raise us to new life through your grace and mercy,
    that our thoughts may ascend to heaven
      and our actions may descend to this earth
        with love and justice.

Words of Assurance (Romans 8, Matthew 13)
God not only knows us but calls us Christ's own.
For all who are led by the Spirit of God
  are children of God.
We need not fall back into fear,
  for we are all God's children,
  invited to shine like the sun
  in the kingdom of heaven!

Passing the Peace of Christ (Romans 8)
Bear witness to one another that we are all indeed children of God. Share signs of peace and adoption with your sisters and brothers in Christ!

Response to the Word (Romans 8, Matthew 13)
Creator and creative God,
  plant us on solid ground.
Nurture us with your wisdom and grace.
Birth in us the hope of your kingdom,
    that we may go forth as your children,
      planting hope and love
        throughout your world.

THANKSGIVING AND COMMUNION

Invitation to the Offering (Matthew 13)

God plants the seeds of love in our hearts. God toils and groans to bring forth creation, and waters the fields of our lives. As we have harvested from God's abundance, let us share God's good gifts with a world in need.

Offering Prayer (Romans 8)

Creator and creative God,
>thank you for entrusting us
>>with your abundance.
Plant in us seeds of generosity,
>that we may nurture your world
>>and spread your grace.
Bless these gifts,
>that they may be planted in places
>>where hope grows dim
>>>and your children groan with need.
In Christ's name, we pray. Amen.

SENDING FORTH

Benediction (Romans 8, Matthew 13)

Creation is waiting for new life and hope.
>**We go into God's world, planting seeds of love.**
Thanks be to God for this glorious gift!

CONTEMPORARY OPTIONS

Gathering Words (Psalm 139)

If we take the wings of the morning,
>God flies alongside.
If we go to the farthest limits of the sea,
>God sails with us there.
If we wander in darkness,
>God offers light for our journey—
>for with God, night is as bright as the day
>and darkness is as light.

Come! Let us follow in God's ways—
    ways that lead to life everlasting.

Praise Sentences (Genesis 28)

Surely God is present here.
Awesome is this place of God's glorious love!
Surely God is present here.
Awesome is this place of God's glorious love!

JULY 24, 2011

Sixth Sunday after Pentecost

Mary J. Scifres

COLOR

Green

SCRIPTURE READINGS

Genesis 29:15-28; Psalm 105:1-11, 45b;
Romans 8:26-39; Matthew 13:31-33, 44-52

THEME IDEAS

It's been said, "good things come to those who wait." Today's scriptures encourage us to trust that God's realm is worth waiting for. Certainly, the hard work of bringing God's realm to fruition is worthy of the effort. Whether working for a beloved wife, trusting in Christ's constant love through times of dire hardship, awaiting the bloom of spring from a small seed, or mixing and kneading flour and yeast into a nourishing loaf of bread, toiling for the sake of love is always worthwhile. When love bursts forth in tangible and life-giving ways, it is always worth the wait. Such bursts of life and love are surely none other than the work of God's realm upon this earth.

INVITATION AND GATHERING

Call to Worship (Psalm 105, Romans 8)

Call to God and sing Christ's praise!
Give thanks to the Lord above!
Seek the Lord and trust God's strength.
Remember God's wonderful works!
Live in the Spirit of love and grace.
Give thanks for Christ's marvelous love!

Opening Prayer (Romans 8, Matthew 13)

Spirit of God,
 you intercede for us
  with sighs too deep for words;
 you search our hearts
  and know our minds.
Set our hearts and minds on you, Holy Spirit,
 that we may know your constant presence
  and everlasting love.
Plant in us a faith that will burst forth into new life,
 that we may be children of your Spirit
  and of Christ's gracious love.

—Or—

Opening Prayer (Matthew 13)

God of the ages,
 we are waiting:
  waiting for grace, waiting for peace,
  waiting for love, waiting for your realm.
Patient and loving God,
 strengthen our faith,
 that our waiting may be transformed
  into hope and action.
Help us be people who know how to wait
 with hope and expectation.
Help us be people who trust your promise
 and your purpose for our lives,
 not only in this time of worship,
  but in the days and weeks and years to come.

PROCLAMATION AND RESPONSE

Prayer of Confession (Psalm 105, Romans 8, Matthew 13)

Loving God,
　　as we seek you,
　　search our hearts.
Root out those places
　　where we are frightened
　　　and unsure of your love.
Forgive us when we give up too easily
　　or refuse to wait for new beginnings.
Help us trust that nothing in all of creation
　　can separate us from you.
Draw us into your arms of love,
　　that we may always know your presence
　　　and rest in your strength.

Words of Assurance (Romans 8)

Remember, beloved children of God,
　　that we are more than conquerors
　　　through Christ who loves us.
Neither angels nor rulers,
　　powers nor principalities,
　　　can take God from us.
Nothing present now or coming in the future
　　can separate God from us.
Dead or alive, sinful or saintly,
　　we are with God!
No height, no depth,
　　nor anything else in all of creation,
　　is able to separate us from the love of God
　　　in Christ Jesus our Savior.
Thanks be to God for this marvelous gift!

Passing the Peace of Christ (Romans 8, Matthew 13)

Waiting and hoping for God's realm to appear, we turn to
one another, sharing signs of this hope and this trust in
our smiles and hugs. Let us share this hope together!

Response to the Word (Genesis 29, Psalm 105, Matthew 13)
> God of possibilities,
>> mold us into people of possibility.
> Keep us ever mindful
>> of your covenant of love and grace.
> Wake us up to watch and wait
>> for your appearance and your guidance.
> Plant in us seeds of life,
>> that we may shine forth as treasures
>>> bright with your love.
> Let your Spirit rise within us,
>> that we may bring forth the kingdom
>>> and influence others to this hope and promise
>>>> in all that we say and do. Amen.

THANKSGIVING AND COMMUNION

Invitation to the Offering (Psalm 105)
> Giving thanks to our God, we share our gifts to make known God's deeds among the peoples. May our gifts and offerings glorify God and tell of Christ's wonderful works!

Offering Prayer (Psalm 105, Matthew 13)
> God of all gifts,
>> thank you for your deeds of love
>>> and for your marvelous works of grace.
> For this earth and its bounty,
>> we give you thanks.
> For our lives and their abundance,
>> we give you praise.
> Bless the gifts we lay before you,
>> that they may be signs of your loving kingdom
>>> to a world awaiting good news.

Communion Prayer (Matthew 13)
 Bakerwoman God,
  bless this gift of bread
   with the yeast of your love.
 Flow through this gift of wine
  with your life-giving grace.
 As we receive these gifts,
  make us one with you
   through the power of your Holy Spirit.
 Nurture our lives,
  that we may be loaves
   of your generous abundance.
 Pour your grace into our hearts,
  that we may be vines of loving nourishment
   for one another and for a world in need
    of growth and strength.
 In Christ's name, we pray. Amen.

SENDING FORTH

Benediction (Romans 8, Matthew 13)
 If God is for us, who is against us?
  **Nothing can separate us
  from Christ's gracious love.**
 If Christ is with us, what can stop us?
  **We go forward now with the strength
  and the power of God.**
 For we are convinced that love is our guide
 and God is our constant companion.
  **We go forth with this promise:
  the kingdom of heaven is here among us now.**

CONTEMPORARY OPTIONS

Gathering Words (Psalm 105, Romans 8)
 What can separate us from the love of Christ?
  Nothing in all the world!

Hunger, hardship, cruelty, troubles?
Nothing in all the world!
Life, death, evil, goodness?
Nothing in all the world!
Angels, devils, rulers, tyrants?
Nothing in all the world!
Indeed, in all these things,
we are more than conquerors
through Christ who loved us
and loves us still.
**Truly, nothing in all the world
can separate us from this love, which is ours
through Christ Jesus our Lord.**
Let us give thanks and praise to God!

—Or—

Gathering Words (Matthew 13)
For a seed to grow,
we are waiting, forever waiting.
For bread to rise,
we are waiting, forever waiting.
For treasure to be found,
we are waiting, forever waiting.
For an oyster to make a pearl,
we are waiting, forever waiting.
For peace to prevail,
we are waiting, forever waiting.
For justice to flow,
we are waiting, forever waiting.
For God's kingdom to come,
we are waiting, forever waiting.

Praise Sentences (Psalm 105)
Call on God's name; sing of Christ's praise.
We give thanks and glory to God!
Call on God's name; sing of Christ's praise.
We give thanks and glory to God!

JULY 31, 2011

Seventh Sunday after Pentecost

Mary J. Scifres

COLOR

Green

SCRIPTURE READINGS

Genesis 32:22-31; Psalm 17:1-7, 15; Romans 9:1-5;
Matthew 14:13-21

THEME IDEAS

Seeing God face to face is a theme that runs through today's very divergent readings. Experiencing God miraculously or directly can bring both joy and fear. After Jacob wrestles all night, he realizes he has seen God face to face and survived. Still, the experience leaves him injured and limping. For the disciples, seeing God's miraculous power in Jesus brings both confusion and joy. Planning to dismiss the crowds as evening descends, the disciples witness loaves and fish transformed into an abundant feast for all. The psalmist cries to God and realizes that beholding God's face brings satisfaction, even in the midst of adversity. Whether we wrestle and struggle, cry out for help, or experience an unexpected miracle, we too can find ourselves satisfied as morning dawns anew and God's amazing presence is revealed.

INVITATION AND GATHERING

Call to Worship (Genesis 32, Psalm 17, Romans 9)
Awake and be satisfied! God is with us this day.
**We cry to God, calling for guidance
and blessing.**
Awake and be satisfied! God is with us now.
We come to Christ, seeking refuge and love.
Awake and be satisfied! Christ is at our side.
**We yearn for the Spirit, searching for truth
and strength.**
Awake and be satisfied! The Spirit dwells within.
**We awaken to a day of blessing!
Thanks be to God!**

Opening Prayer (Genesis 32, Psalm 17, Romans 9)
God of ages past and days to come,
hear us as we come into your presence.
Show us your steadfast love
and guide us in your mysterious ways.
Invite us to look upon your radiant face
with humility and hope,
that our faces may be filled with your radiant love,
and our lives might shine forth
with your wisdom and truth.
In the power of the Holy Spirit, we pray. Amen.

—Or—

Opening Prayer (Matthew 14)
God of our hopes and dreams,
we are empty and long to be filled;
we are hungry and long to be fed;
we are lost and long to be found.
Gather us into your love,
and pick up the pieces of our lives,
just as Jesus gathered up the fragments
that remained after feeding the crowds.

Call us anew to eat our fill
    and find our true nourishment in Jesus,
        the bread of life and hope of the ages. Amen.
(B. J. Beu)

PROCLAMATION AND RESPONSE

Prayer of Confession (Genesis 32, Psalm 17)
O Morning Star,
    as day is breaking,
        may the fears of the night fade away.
Grant us the courage to look upon your face
    and the wisdom to acknowledge the many ways
        we need your grace.
Test us, and try our hearts.
Cleanse away our sin and despair.
Cast away any thoughts of wickedness,
    and hold us fast to your ways
        of righteousness and love.
Incline your ear and hear us
    as we call to you, O God.
Be our refuge and our strength,
    that we may be a people of hope,
        born anew in your merciful grace. Amen.

Words of Assurance (Psalm 17, Matthew 14)
Awake to the good news of God's love:
    In the name of Jesus Christ, we are forgiven
    and fed by God's gracious hand.

Preparing to Hear the Word (Genesis 32, Psalm 17, Matthew 14)
Compassionate God, feed us with your word. Awaken us
with your Spirit. In this time of listening and reflecting,
may we see your loving face and know your guiding wisdom. Amen.

Response to the Word (Genesis 32, Psalm 17, Matthew 14)
> Gracious God,
> > help us integrate the mystery of your presence
> > > into our very being.
> Where there is hunger,
> > may we offer nourishment.
> Where there is confusion,
> > may we offer light.
> Where there is despair,
> > may we offer hope.
> Shine through us,
> > that your face may be seen in our very lives. Amen.

THANKSGIVING AND COMMUNION

Invitation to the Offering (Matthew 14)
> As Jesus fed the crowds with only a few loaves and a couple of fish, God now invites us to gather our gifts to care for God's world. As we share generously, Christ will multiply these gifts into an abundant feast.

Offering Prayer (Matthew 14)
> Compassionate God,
> > bless these gifts with your grace.
> May they become loaves of bread
> > for those who are hungry
> > > and guiding lights
> > > > for those who are lost.
> May they become signs of hope
> > for those in despair
> > > and symbols of love
> > > > for all to know.
> In Christ's name, we pray. Amen.

Invitation to Communion (Genesis 32, Matthew 14)
> Come to the table, you who are scattered and torn.
> > **Here we find hope.**
> Come to the table, you who are scared and lonely.
> > **Here we find love.**

Come to the table, you who are tired and tense.
Here we find rest for our souls
and food for our journey.
Come to the table, you who are lost and are searching.
Here we discover guidance
and light in our darkness.
Come to the table, you who are happy or sad.
Here our lives are embraced by God's grace.
(Joanne Carlson Brown)

The Great Thanksgiving (Genesis 32, Matthew 14)

It is right and a good and joyful thing,
always and everywhere, to give thanks to you,
Mighty God, our Comforter and Sustainer.
You made us in your image, to love and be loved.
When our love failed, your love remained steadfast.
You delivered us from captivity in Egypt,
made covenant, time and again, to be our God,
that we might be your people.
In the lineage of Abraham and Sarah,
Isaac and Rebekah, Jacob and Rachel,
we come now with gratitude and praise
as we awaken anew to the amazing mystery
of your presence and your covenant of love.
And so, with your people on earth,
and all the company of heaven,
we praise your name
and join their unending hymn.
Holy, holy, holy Lord, God of power and might,
heaven and earth are full of your glory.
Hosanna in the highest. Blessed is the One
who comes in the name of the Lord.
Hosanna in the highest.

Holy are you, and blessed is your Son, Jesus Christ.
As Jesus walked among us on this earth,
he offered healing and mercy to the sick,
food and nourishment to the hungry,
and loving compassion to all in need.

Through Christ and the Holy Spirit,
  you gave birth to the church,
  delivered us from slavery to sin and death,
  and made with us a new covenant
  by water and the Spirit.

You call us this day to awaken to your presence,
  to wrestle with our calling,
  to be your compassion in the world,
  and to speak the truth of your love.
As we come to the table, you nurture us to live
  with bread that always fills
  and living water that always satisfies.

We remember the evening when Jesus fed thousands
  from only a few loaves and fish,
  and that last night when Jesus ate with his disciples,
  taking and breaking bread, blessing it,
  and giving it with these words,
  "Take, eat; this is my body."
We remember that Jesus took the cup also,
  blessing it, giving thanks to you,
  and reminding all of us that this is his life
  poured out for all of us—
  your love living in all of us,
  your Spirit's nurture flowing through our lives.

And so, in remembrance of these,
  your mighty acts in Christ Jesus,
  we offer ourselves in praise and thanksgiving
  as a holy and living gift to you and to your world.
In union with Christ's gift of love
  to us and to your world,
  we proclaim the mystery of faith.
  Christ has died.
  Christ is risen.
  Christ will come again.

Communion Prayer (Matthew 14)
Pour out your Holy Spirit
on us and on these gifts of bread and wine.
Make them be for us the life and love of Christ,
that we may be for the world, disciples of Christ,
redeemed by your love and fed by your grace.
Awaken us with your Spirit,
that we may be one with Christ,
one with each other,
and one in ministry to all the world.
Shine upon our lives,
that we may we proclaim your love,
feed the hungry, and show compassion to all,
until Christ comes in final victory
and we feast at your heavenly banquet.
Through Jesus the Christ,
together with the Holy Spirit,
all honor and glory is yours, almighty God,
now and forevermore. Amen.

SENDING FORTH

Benediction (Genesis 32, Matthew 14)
Behold, we have seen the face of God!
We have heard the good news of Christ!
Go forth with the power of the Holy Spirit!
We go forth to bless the world!

CONTEMPORARY OPTIONS

Gathering Words (Genesis 32, Psalm 17, Matthew 14)
Wrestling through the night,
we wonder if morning will ever come.
Awake and see the light of God!
Wrestling with doubts,
we wonder if we will ever find certainty.
Awake and see the light of God!

Wrestling with hunger and thirst,
we yearn to be filled with good things.
Awake and see the light of God!
Wrestling with our call,
we wonder which way to go.
Awake and see the light of God!
Wrestling, waiting, wondering,
we are fed by Christ's mercy and grace.
Awake and see the light of God!

Praise Sentences (Genesis 32, Matthew 14)
God's love and grace are here!
God's love and grace are here!
Give thanks and endless praise!
Give thanks and endless praise!

AUGUST 7, 2011

Eighth Sunday after Pentecost
B. J. Beu

COLOR
Green

SCRIPTURE READINGS
Genesis 37:1-4, 12-28; Psalm 105:1-6, 16-22, 45b;
Romans 10:5-15; Matthew 14:22-33

THEME IDEAS
Even in the midst of our failings, God can turn human
weakness into acts of deliverance. Genesis 37 begins the
story of Joseph's sale into slavery by his brothers. Psalm
105 proclaims that God used this act of human betrayal to
deliver all the lands from the effects of famine. Paul proclaims that all who profess Christ with their lips and believe in him with their whole hearts will be saved.
Matthew 14 recalls the story of Peter's fear and doubt as
he walks on the water toward Jesus. Jesus rescues Peter
from the sea and admonishes him for his doubts.

INVITATION AND GATHERING

Call to Worship (Genesis 37, Psalm 105, Romans 10)
Give thanks to the Lord.
Call on God's holy name.
Rejoice in the Lord.

God fills our hearts with joy.
Give thanks to the Lord.
Proclaim God's mighty works.
Rejoice in the Lord.
God's miracles are a wonder to behold.
Give thanks to the Lord.
Trust in God's salvation.
Rejoice in the Lord.
God turns even our failings into glory.

Opening Prayer (Genesis 37, Psalm 105, Romans 10:15, Matthew 14)

Eternal God,
you visit us in dreams,
offering us glimpses of new possibilities;
you rescue us from life's storms,
lifting us out of the raging waters.
Be with us now
as we call on your name.
Reveal your purposes for our world,
that we may be of use and service.
Bless us with the courage to spread your word,
that it may be said of us:
"How beautiful are the feet
of those who bring good news!"

PROCLAMATION AND RESPONSE

Prayer of Confession (Genesis 37, Matthew 14)

God of infinite possibilities,
we are like a boat that is beaten by the storm:
without your aid we are powerless
to get where we are going;
we are like disciples who sit in fear for their lives:
without your presence we are trapped
within the prison of our feelings
of helplessness;

we are like those lost in wonder and disbelief:
    without your assurance we quickly drown
        in our hopelessness and despair.
Grant us the courage of Peter
    to believe that through your power
        anything is possible.
Give us the confidence of Joseph
    to live as dreamers,
        even when the world turns against us,
        that we may always be found faithful. Amen.

Assurance of Pardon (Romans 10:11, 13)

Christ's love is greater than our deepest failings.
    "The scripture says, 'No one who believes in him
        will be put to shame.' "
    "For, 'Everyone who calls on the name of the Lord
        shall be saved.' "

Response to the Word (Romans 10:14-15)

We live in a world full of people who know more of Santa
Clauses and Easter Bunnies than they do of mangers and
empty tombs. We live amongst neighbors who hunger for
spiritual truth but do not know where it may be found.
Paul's question is as true today as it was 2,000 years ago:
"How are they to believe in one of whom they have never
heard? And how are they to hear without someone to proclaim him? . . . As it is written, 'How beautiful are the feet
of those who bring good news!' "

THANKSGIVING AND COMMUNION

Offering Prayer (Genesis 37, Psalm 105)

Loving God,
    though his own brothers threw him into a pit
        and sold him into slavery,
            Joseph remained faithful;
    though his feet were bound with chains
        and his neck with a collar of iron,
            Joseph placed his fate in your hands.

May our lives reflect this same devotion
in all our endeavors.
And may our offering be a sign
of our faithfulness to you, O God,
our savior and deliverer. Amen.

SENDING FORTH

Benediction (Psalm 105, Matthew 14)
God blesses us with strength for the journey.
Our hearts sing God's praises.
Christ lifts us up from the raging waters of life.
Our spirits rejoice in our salvation.
The Spirit guides us with dreams full of hope
and promise.
Our lives rest secure in the One who is faithful.
Thanks be to God!

CONTEMPORARY OPTIONS

Gathering Words (Matthew 14)
Jesus walks to us over the water.
"Call to us Lord. We long to be with you."
Jesus calls to us, "Come! Do not be afraid."
"Save us Lord, we're sinking!"
Jesus saves us from our fears.
God delivers us from the storm.
Thanks be to God!

Praise Sentences (Psalm 105)
Praise the Lord!
Call on God's holy name.
Praise God with singing.
Praise God's wonderful works.
Rejoice in God with all your heart.
Delight in God's miracles.
Praise the Lord!
Praise the Lord!
Praise the Lord!

AUGUST 14, 2011

Ninth Sunday after Pentecost

B. J. Beu

COLOR

Green

SCRIPTURE READINGS

Genesis 45:1-15; Psalm 133; Romans 11:1-2a, 29-32;
Matthew 15:(10-20) 21-28

THEME IDEAS

What unites us is far greater than what divides us. Joseph
forgives his brothers for selling him into slavery, for God
used this terrible act to save Israelites and Egyptians alike
from famine. The psalmist celebrates when kindred live
together in unity. Paul asks rhetorically whether God has
rejected the Hebrew people by offering salvation to the
Gentiles, and answers no. Jesus initially refuses to help a
Canaanite woman's daughter until the woman presses her
case. Then Jesus joyfully heals the daughter, marveling at
the mother's faith. We are all bound together in the un-
conditional love of God.

INVITATION AND GATHERING

*Call to Worship (Genesis 45, Psalm 133, Romans 11,
Matthew 15)*
(*Feel free to substitute "Holy One" or another God reference for
"O Lord."*)

When hatred and division separate us, O Lord,
your love binds us together.
When past quarrels estrange us from one another,
your love binds us together.
When we feel excluded and left out,
your love binds us together.
When we seek to keep your love for ourselves,
your love binds us together.
Bind us together, O Lord.
Bind us together.

Opening Prayer (Genesis 45, Psalm 133, Romans 11, Matthew 15)

Eternal God,
part the veil that blinds us to our unity.
When our families hurt and betray us,
help us find ways to let go of our pain
and work for the healing of all people.
When we feel abandoned by those we love,
help us trust in the power of forgiveness
and seek to bring peace and reconciliation.
When our hearts are pierced with anguish,
help us reach out to those who can bring us solace
and find in the search, grace upon grace,
through your loving Spirit. Amen.

PROCLAMATION AND RESPONSE

Prayer of Confession (Genesis 45, Psalm 133, Matthew 15)

Merciful God,
we would rather be the Joseph
who ruled all of Egypt
with unquestioned power and authority,
than the Joseph
who wept with perfect forgiveness
on the necks of the brothers
who had sold him into slavery;

we would rather be the disciples
who felt superior to the Canaanite woman
when Jesus rebuffed her plea for help,
than the disciples
after Jesus healed the woman's child
when confronted by her faith.
Forgive us, O God,
when we try to keep your love for ourselves.
Help us know the joy of living in unity,
even with those we would rather live without.

Assurance of Pardon (Romans 11:29)
The gifts and calling of God are irrevocable.
Rejoice in the knowledge of God's saving love.

Response to the Word (Genesis 45, Psalm 133, Romans 11, Matthew 15)
Even in the midst of apparent tragedy,
God is at work, preserving a remnant.
Thanks be to God!
Even in the midst of apparent rejection,
God is at work, saving the faithful.
Thanks be to God!
Even in the midst of apparent insult,
God is calling us to stand up for ourselves
and those we love.
Thanks be to God!
God challenges us to look beneath our differences
and live together in unity.
Thanks be to God!

THANKSGIVING AND COMMUNION

Offering Prayer (Genesis 22)
Bountiful God,
when famine threatened the world,
you blessed Joseph with dreams
that would save all your children;

when hunger threatens our world,
   you bless us with dreams
      that we can save all your children.
When our dreams are your dreams, Holy One,
   the world is truly blessed.
Accept these gifts
   as tokens of our dreams and yours
      that we all may be one. Amen.

SENDING FORTH

Benediction (Genesis 22, Romans 6)
The God of dreams has brought us together.
The God of dreams seals us in love.
The God of love has knit us together in unity.
The God of love heals all divisions.
The God of all people sends us forth together.
Our God brings us home.

CONTEMPORARY OPTIONS

Gathering Words (Psalm 133)
Hey, everybody, live together in unity.
We'll love one another as friends should.
Pull together as family.
It's awesome when we live as God intends.

Praise Sentences (Psalm 13)
Our God is merciful.
Praise the God of our salvation.
Our God is just.
Praise the God of our salvation.
Our God creates us as sisters and brothers.
Praise the God of our salvation.
Praise the God of our salvation.
Praise the God of our salvation.

AUGUST 21, 2011

Tenth Sunday after Pentecost
Mary Petrina Boyd

COLOR

Green

SCRIPTURE READINGS

Exodus 1:8–2:10; Psalm 124; Romans 12:1-8;
Matthew 16:13-20

THEME IDEAS

The life of faith is lived in community, where many gifts
support the body of Christ. In the Exodus account,
women work together to oppose injustice and protect life.
The midwives disobey Pharaoh and call forth new life.
Moses lives because of his mother, sister, and the daughter of Pharaoh. In Matthew, Peter names Jesus for who he
is, and a new community, the church, begins to take root.
Paul names the differing gifts that support the community, the body of Christ.

INVITATION AND GATHERING

Call to Worship (Psalm 124)
Our help is in the name of the Lord,
who made heaven and earth.
    We belong to God.
When we feel overwhelmed,

God is on our side.
When we are afraid,
God will keep us safe.
Our help is in the name of the Lord,
who made heaven and earth.
Blessed be the Lord!

Opening Prayer (Romans 12)

Loving God,
call us together as your people;
transform us with your love.
Transform our hearts,
that we may love generously.
Transform our eyes,
that we may see your grace.
Transform our hands,
that we may serve others.
Transform our spirits,
that we may be the body of Christ,
gathered to worship
and sent out to serve. Amen.

PROCLAMATION AND RESPONSE

Prayer of Confession (Exodus 1–2, Romans 12)

Caring God,
you call us to be the body of Christ:
to live in community,
to care for one another,
to use our different gifts.
Instead of working to sustain community,
we follow our own desires.
Instead of trusting in your care,
we think we can do it alone.
Forgive our neglect of others.
Give us obedient spirits,
that we may care for one another,
depend on your love,
and use our gifts for your gospel. Amen.

Words of Assurance (Psalm 124, Romans 12)
> The Lord is on our side,
>> offering words of forgiveness,
>> protecting us from danger.
> We are a forgiven people,
>> bound together in God's love.
> We are the body of Christ, forgiven and free.

Passing the Peace of Christ (Romans 12)
> Jesus is the Messiah, the hope of the world, the one who brings us the gift of peace. Look into the eyes of your neighbor and see the light of Christ reflected there. Recognize each other as the body of Christ. Share Christ's peace with one another.

Response to the Word (Romans 12)
> God of love,
>> open our hearts to each other.
> Give us the courage to resist oppression.
> Help us protect the world from evil.
> Give us the wisdom to see ourselves as we truly are.
> Give us the vision to see you and hear your voice.
> Give us the courage to answer your call
> Grant us the endurance to use our gifts
>> for the purpose of your realm.
> Work your transforming love within us
>> that we may know your will
>>> and serve you with joy. Amen.

THANKSGIVING AND COMMUNION

Invitation to the Offering (Romans 12)
> God has blessed us with an abundance of gifts. We are called to offer all that we are to God—our bodies, our spirits, our minds, our time, and our money. As the body of Christ, we are called to be in ministry with others. With true generosity, let us give of ourselves this morning.

Offering Prayer (Romans 12)
> Generous God,
>> you have given us many gifts
>>> and drawn us together into Christ's body,
>>> the church.
>> You have blessed us
>>> with generous and cheerful spirits.
>> May the gifts of our money, time, and talents
>>> support the ministry of your church. Amen.

Invitation to Communion (Romans 12)
> Here at the table, we see most clearly that we are part of
> the body of Christ. We are no longer divided into people
> of different ages, different ideas, different backgrounds,
> different gifts. Here unique individuals become a single
> body, made richer for the multitude of gifts shared. Here,
> we feast on one bread and one cup, and become one body
> in service to the world.

SENDING FORTH

Benediction (Exodus 1–2, Psalm 127)
> Resist the powers that use people.
> Hear the cries of the weak.
> Dare to work for justice.
> Know that God—Source, Word, and Spirit—
>> is your help, will keep you safe,
>> and will bring you new life.
> You are blessed by God and sent to serve.

CONTEMPORARY OPTIONS

Gathering Words (Matthew 16)
> Who is this man?
> **This is Jesus!**
> Who is this man?
> **This is the Messiah!**
> Who is this man?
> **This is the child of the living God!**

Praise Sentences (Psalm 124)

The Lord is on our side!
We fear nothing.
God is our help.
Blessed be the Lord.

AUGUST 28, 2011

Eleventh Sunday after Pentecost

Laura Jaquith Bartlett

COLOR

Green

SCRIPTURE READINGS

Exodus 3:1-15; Psalm 105:1-6, 23-26, 45c;
Romans 12:9-21; Matthew 16:21-28

THEME IDEAS

Just when we think we have God figured out, God over-
turns our expectations once again. God takes an inarticu-
late, excuse-riddled murderer and turns him into one of the
greatest leaders of the Hebrew people. Writing in Romans,
Paul (who has a life-changing story to rival that of Moses)
gives us an upside-down recipe for living in Christ: "Do
not be overcome by evil, but overcome evil with good."
Meanwhile, Jesus reminds us of one of the greatest, and
most difficult, paradoxes of Christianity: to save your life
you must first lose it. So we find ourselves once again surprised by the limitless and inexplicable nature of God's
love, and we rejoice to stand together on holy ground.

INVITATION AND GATHERING

Call to Worship (Psalm 105)

Give thanks for all the wonderful works of God.

Praise the Lord!

Sing a new song of praise to the God of all peoples.
Praise the Lord!
Proclaim God's name to all the world.
Praise the Lord!
We are God's chosen people; God is with us always.
Praise the Lord!
Let our hearts rejoice, for the Lord is God.
Praise the Lord!

Opening Prayer (Exodus 3, Romans 12, Matthew 16)
Surprising God,
you have an uncomfortable habit
of showing up where we least expect you:
in a burning bush,
in the face of an enemy,
in a livestock feed trough,
on a rough wooden cross.
Turn our lives upside down
with your radical love.
Help us fully embrace your surprises,
even as we revel in the joy
of being fully embraced
by your all-encompassing grace
and mercy.
We pray in the name
of your most amazing surprise of all:
your Son, Jesus Christ. Amen.

PROCLAMATION AND RESPONSE

Prayer of Confession (Exodus 3, Romans 12, Matthew 16)
God of Mystery,
we are constantly amazed
by the depth and breadth of your love.
Over and over again,
you turn our expectations inside out
and upside down.

And still we don't understand
   the radical nature of your grace.
We play by our own rules of justice,
      even when it means excluding those
         we are called to love and defend.
In our darkest moments,
   we doubt if we are worthy of your trust.
God, help us remember
      that you give us all the tools we need;
      that through the solid foundation of your love,
      we find the strength to follow your call
         as true disciples of Jesus Christ.
Surprise us again, O God.
Surprise us again.

Words of Assurance (Exodus 3, Psalm 105)

The God who brought our ancestors out of slavery
   will not desert us.
God has promised to be with us
   throughout all generations.
Let the hearts of those who seek the Lord rejoice,
   for God is with us!

Passing the Peace of Christ

Rejoice, for you are standing on holy ground.
   Praise the Lord!

Response to the Word (Exodus 3, Romans 12, Matthew 16)

Moses was a murderer,
   **yet you turned him into a hero
   who led his people to freedom.**
Moses couldn't speak well,
   **yet you put words in his mouth
   to argue his people's cause before Pharaoh.**
We are taught to attack our enemies,
   **yet you teach us to bless those
   who persecute us.**

We are overcome by evil,
yet you tell us to overcome evil with good.
Jesus is the savior of the world,
**yet the crucifixion tells the story of a man
who could not even save himself.**
We desperately want to save our own lives.
**God of Paradox, help us understand
how to lose our lives in order to save them.**

THANKSGIVING AND COMMUNION

Offering Prayer (Matthew 16)
Dear God,
we offer you now these gifts.
Take our money and use it
to bring comfort to those in need.
Take our service and use it
to bring justice to those who are oppressed.
Take our witness and use it
to bring good news to those who hunger
for hope.
Take our lives and use them
for our very salvation.
We pray through Jesus Christ,
the one whom we follow
even to the cross. Amen.

SENDING FORTH

Benediction (Exodus 3)
God promised to be with Moses, and we are here to witness to the fulfillment of that promise. From generation to
generation, the God of Israel is also the God of *(your community's name)*. The God of the burning bush is waiting
even now to encounter you, call you, challenge you, and
change you. Go out to be sustained and surprised by the
love of God. Amen.

CONTEMPORARY OPTIONS

Gathering Words (Exodus 3, Matthew 16)
God calls us from a burning bush.
We are standing on holy ground!
The Spirit calls us to proclaim God's name
to all generations.
We are standing on holy ground!
Jesus calls us from the cross: come and follow me.
We are standing on holy ground!

Praise Sentences (Exodus 3)
God declares, "I AM WHO I AM."
The God of our ancestors is with us today.
God is our God, from generation to generation.
Let us worship God on this holy ground!
Let us worship God on this holy ground!

SEPTEMBER 4, 2011

Twelfth Sunday after Pentecost
B. J. Beu

COLOR
Green

SCRIPTURE READINGS
Exodus 12:1-14; Psalm 149 (or Psalm 148); Romans 13:8-14; Matthew 18:15-20

THEME IDEAS
Love and judgment focus today's readings. In Exodus, God's love for the Hebrew people leads to God's judgment against their Egyptian slave holders—an act of love and judgment commemorated in the institution of the Passover celebration. In Psalm 149, God's love for the weak and the helpless leads to God's judgment against unjust kings and nobles—an act of love and judgment leading to the psalmist's call to celebrate God's salvation with music. In Romans, Paul speaks about the commandment to love as a fulfillment of the law. In John, Jesus' procedure for dealing with sin in the church ensures that future reconciliation will not be encumbered by gossip from unaffected parties.

INVITATION AND GATHERING

Call to Worship (Psalm 149)
Praise the Lord! Sing to the Lord a new song.
Let all God's children rejoice!

195

Clap your hands and praise God with dancing.
Shout for joy and praise God with music.
For God brings justice to the peoples.
God brings judgment upon the powerful.
Praise the Lord! Sing to the Lord a new song.
Let all God's children rejoice!

Opening Prayer (Exodus 12, Psalm 149, Romans 13)

God of love and judgment,
> when the Egyptians enslaved the Hebrew people,
>> your love set them free;
> when rulers oppress the poor and powerless,
>> your judgment brings peace and justice
>>> back to the land.
Move us, O God,
> that we may fulfill the law of love
> and be a people who radiate your light.
Touch our hearts,
> that we may come to love our neighbor
> as we come to love ourselves. Amen.

PROCLAMATION AND RESPONSE

Prayer of Confession (Genesis 29, Romans 8)

Merciful God,
> it is easier to destroy than it is to build;
> it is easier to hurt than it is to heal.
Forgive us, Holy One,
> when we parade our wounds for all to see,
>> rather than work quietly for forgiveness
>> and reconciliation.
Correct us, Gracious Spirit,
> when we seek public vindication of our wrongs
>> over the health of your body.
Help us love one another with a perfect love,
> that we may cast aside the works of darkness
> and fulfill the law of love. Amen.

Words of Assurance (Matthew 18:20, Romans 13)
Hear the words of Jesus:
"Where two or three are gathered in my name,
I am there among them."
As we gather to fulfill the law of love,
Christ is here with us and we are made whole.

Response to the Word (Romans 13)
Morning has dawned.
Christ's light shines upon us.
It's time to wake up.
For salvation is nearer to us now
than when we first became believers.
**Lay aside the works of darkness
and put on the armor of light.**
It's time to wake up.
Christ's light shines upon us.

THANKSGIVING AND COMMUNION

Offering Prayer (Romans 8, Matthew 13)
In celebration of their deliverance from slavery,
and gratitude for their freedom,
the ancient Hebrews offered you their worship
and their praise.
In celebration of our deliverance
from the things that enslave us
and gratitude for your saving love,
we offer you our worship and our praise.
Just as the Passover stands as a perpetual observance
of our thanksgiving for your love and care,
so may our offerings be a perpetual observance
of our gratitude for your calling in Jesus Christ.
Amen.

SENDING FORTH

Benediction (Psalm 149)
God has put a new song in our hearts.
Sing a new song to the Lord.

The judgment of God brings victory to the righteous.
Sing a new song to the Lord.
The love of God has set us free.
Sing a new song to the Lord.

CONTEMPORARY OPTIONS

Gathering Words (Romans 13)

Have you heard the good news?
**When Christ is with us,
we're a people of love and light.**
Have you felt the good news?
**When Christ heals us,
we touch God's love and light.**
Have you lived the good news?
**When we're gathered in Christ's name,
we are God's love and light.**

Praise Sentences (Psalm 149)

Praise the Lord!
Sing to the Lord a new song.
Rejoice in our God.
Praise God with dancing, with music and voice.
Praise the Lord!
Sing to the Lord a new song.
Praise the Lord!

SEPTEMBER 11, 2011

Thirteenth Sunday after Pentecost
Matthew J. Packer

COLOR

Green

SCRIPTURE READINGS

Exodus 14:19-31; Exodus 15:1b-11, 20-21;
Romans 14:1-12; Matthew 18:21-35

THEME IDEAS

The passages from Exodus and Matthew share the theme
of deliverance. Neither the Israelites nor the slave in Jesus'
parable do anything to earn their deliverance—it is offered in grace and mercy. The Israelites respond with a
song of praise to God. The slave, however, does not show
grace or mercy and is punished. Romans offers a theme
of being set apart. Just as we have received grace, mercy,
and forgiveness, we, who are in Christ, are set apart to do
likewise.

INVITATION AND GATHERING

Call to Worship (Exodus 15)
O Lord, majestic in holiness, who is like you?
**In the greatness of your majesty
you overthrew your adversaries.**
O Lord, awesome in splendor, who is like you?

**Your right hand, O Lord, glorious in power,
shattered the enemy.**
O Lord, worker of wonders, who is like you?
**Sing to the Lord, my strength and my might,
you are my salvation!**

Opening Prayer (Romans 12)
In this moment, gracious God,
you have called us away from the world
to a place and a time
where we can commune with you
and with one another.
Hallow this communion, we pray.
Calm our anxious spirits,
that we may be set apart
to hear your word of truth
through which we receive grace
to bring about the obedience of faith.
Open us to the reality of your all-embracing love,
both in this place and in the wider world.
May we, by our words and actions,
be bearers of your kingdom,
in the name and Spirit of the Christ. Amen.

PROCLAMATION AND RESPONSE

Prayer of Confession (Matthew 18, Romans 12)
Lord,
your grace and mercy are ever-present in our lives,
your forgiveness is boundless in mercy
when we fail to live in Christlike ways.
And yet, we are quick to carry a grudge—
quick to find fault,
quick to assign blame,
quick to harden our hearts toward others.
Set us apart, loving God,
to extend and model the grace you have shown us
by offering grace to others.

We pray in the name of the One who died
so that we might fully live. Amen.

Words of Assurance (Matthew 18, Exodus 15)

As Christ has forgiven us, we are to forgive others.
In the name of Jesus Christ, you are forgiven.
In the name of Jesus Christ, you are forgiven.
Praise to God who has triumphed gloriously. Amen.

Passing the Peace of Christ

Now is the time to share Christ's love and forgiveness
with one another. Let the Christ in you greet the Christ in
another with signs of peace and reconciliation.

Response to the Word (Matthew 18)

As we have heard, so may we respond. Transform our
thinking and our doing, O God. May our actions speak
your mercy, and may our lives speak your generous love.
Amen.

THANKSGIVING AND COMMUNION

Invitation to the Offering (Matthew 18)

In Jesus' parable, the king forgave a debt that could never
be repaid. The slave responded by withholding mercy to
his own debtor. How fortunate we are that our God is like
the king and not the slave! As we give today, may we do
so out of the lavishness we have been shown by a God
who forgives and loves us beyond measure.

Offering Prayer (Matthew 18)

Giving God,
all we are and all we have
come from you.
We offer back to you
what has always been yours.
As you have entrusted your gifts to us,
so we return these gifts to you,
trusting that you will multiply them
to the great glory of your kingdom on earth.

We pray through Jesus
who gave the totality of his life for us. Amen.

SENDING FORTH

Benediction (Exodus 14)
Go with the God who can part
the troubled waters of your life
and lead you through to dry ground.
Go with the God who can scatter and subdue
all that hinders you on your journey.
Go forth in God's might and in God's peace. Amen.

CONTEMPORARY OPTIONS

Gathering Words (Exodus 15)
Who is like you, O Lord, majestic in holiness
and awesome in splendor?
**We will sing to the Lord,
for God has triumphed gloriously.
God is our strength, our might,
and our salvation!**

Praise Sentences (Exodus 15)
This is my God, whom I will praise,
the God of my mothers and fathers,
the God whom I exalt.
**The Lord is mighty
and holy is God's name!**

SEPTEMBER 18, 2011

Fourteenth Sunday after Pentecost
Hans Holznagel

COLOR

Green

SCRIPTURE READINGS

Exodus 16:2-15; Psalm 105:1-6, 37-45; Philippians 1:21-30;
Matthew 20:1-16

THEME IDEAS

To complain is human. It can also be biblical. In the
wilderness, the "whole congregation" complains to Moses
and Aaron and is mystified by God's abundant, nourishing reply. From prison, Paul honestly confesses his sadness and struggles in solidarity with the Philippians to
encourage them in joyful perseverance. In Jesus' parable,
the laborers' apparently reasonable wage-and-hour com-
plaint prompts the landowner to defend his right to pay
the last first—causing Jesus' audience, no doubt, to ponder a realm in which their own assumptions about rules,
roles, and status are challenged. Far from idle grumbling,
legitimate complaints that are raised and heard with care
may further faithful relationships and even produce unexpected answers.

INVITATION AND GATHERING

Call to Worship (Psalm 105, Matthew 20)
Descendants of Abraham and Sarah,
> remember the wonderful works of God:
>> miracles, judgments, and abundance,
>> food from heaven, water in the desert,
>> words to live by.

Ponder God's realm of statutes and laws,
> of covenant kept in surprising ways.

Ponder a realm where the last are first.
Remember the wonderful works of God.

Opening Prayer (Exodus 16, Psalm 105)
Hungry, we seek nourishment,
> as we wander in the wilderness of our lives.

Comfortable, we seek assurance,
> as we search for the challenge of authenticity.

Center our hearts on right relationships with you,
> with one another, and with your created world,
>> that we may be instruments of your realm
>> on earth as in heaven. Amen.

PROCLAMATION AND RESPONSE

Prayer of Confession (Exodus 16, Matthew 20)
God of life and wisdom,
> we lay before you the idle grumblings
>> that often overtake us.

When daily annoyances come,
> may we be aware enough of your abundance
>> that joy may overcome bitterness.

Where we have real complaints,
> grant us first the grace of self-examination
>> and then the gifts of careful, honest speech
>> and listening hearts.

And when the answer is unexpected—
  like manna instead of fleshpots,
    or the last paid first—
      help us discern the signs, wonders,
        habits, and ways of your coming realm.
In Christ's name we pray. Amen.

Words of Assurance (Exodus 16, Psalm 105:3b)
"Let the hearts of those who seek the LORD rejoice,"
  says the psalmist.
We know our God can bear our confessions,
  for nothing can separate us from the love of God,
  which we know in Christ Jesus.
In that love, we are forgiven.
Let the whole congregation say,
  Amen.

Unison Response to the Word (Exodus 16, Psalm 105)
The word of God is like bread from heaven.
May we remember God's holy promises
  and make known God's deeds among the peoples.
Amen.

THANKSGIVING AND COMMUNION

Invitation to the Offering (Psalm 105)
God's abundant generosity is like water gushing from a rock, flowing through the desert like a river. Let us respond to God's love by giving back a portion of what we have as we present our tithes and offerings.

Offering Prayer (Philippians 1, Matthew 20)
Gracious God,
  accept these gifts,
    as fruits of our own labor.
May these gifts be our prayer
  for the fruitful labor of the church,
  for progress and joy in faith,
  for the coming of your realm
    in all creation. Amen.

SENDING FORTH

Benediction (Philippians 1, Matthew 20)
Live your life in a manner worthy
    of the gospel of Christ:
        standing firm in one spirit,
        striving side by side with one mind,
        watching for signs of the realm of God.
Go in peace. Amen.

CONTEMPORARY OPTIONS

Gathering Words (Exodus 16, Psalm 105, Philippians 1, Matthew 20)
Sisters and brothers,
    welcome to this household of faith.
Come from your desert wandering and field laboring.
Come justice-wondering and bread-hungering,
    joy-savoring and faith-striving.
God has brought us out and brought us in
    with joy and singing.
Praise God!

Praise Sentences (Psalm 105, Matthew 20)
The realm of God is like this:
the last will be first and the first will be last.
    Give thanks to God.
    Make known God's deeds.
    Call on God's name.
God's abundance is heavenly food,
revealed as the morning dew rises.
    Sing to God, sing praises to God.
    Tell of God's wonderful works.
    Let those who seek God rejoice!

SEPTEMBER 25, 2011

Fifteenth Sunday after Pentecost
Mary J. Scifres

COLOR
Green

SCRIPTURE READINGS
Exodus 17:1-7; Psalm 78:1-4, 12-16; Philippians 2:1-13;
Matthew 21:23-32

THEME IDEAS
God's authority emerges in readings from Exodus and
Matthew today, but Philippians' focus on the mind of
Christ reminds us that God's authority was displayed in
Jesus through his humble servanthood. The call to serve is
always from God and is an opportunity to live as Christ's
followers. Whether we are serving water to the thirsty,
teaching God's great works to the uninitiated, loving our
neighbors with compassion, or working in the fields of
God's world, when we do so in answer to God's call, we
are doing so by God's authority.

INVITATION AND GATHERING

Call to Worship (Psalm 72)
Give ear to God's teaching. Listen to God's words.
We gather to hear stories of old.
Give voice to God's glory. Sing of God's deeds.

We gather to sing praises to God.
Prepare for God's work. Answer Christ's call.
**We listen and learn, worship and praise,
in order to serve in God's world.**

Opening Prayer (Exodus 17, Philippians 2)
We gather in your presence, Christ of compassion,
   thirsting for your living water.
Flow through this time of worship
   with your grace and wisdom.
Nourish us with words of truth and challenge.
Strengthen us to go forth in humility and love
   as your servants working in the world.

PROCLAMATION AND RESPONSE

Prayer of Confession (Exodus 17, Psalm 78, Philippians 2, Matthew 21)
God of ages past and days to come,
   when we grumble and groan,
      we are like children of the Exodus;
   when we doubt your authority
      and question your call,
         we are like priests and elders of old.
Forgive us.
Make us new in your grace,
   and clothe us with your compassion.
Open our eyes to your presence
   and our minds to your guidance,
      that we may have the very mind of Christ.
In Christ's holy name, we pray. Amen.

Words of Assurance (Psalm 78, Matthew 21)
Give ear to Christ's promise:
   God's realm is open to all—
      tax collectors and prostitutes,
      sinners and slackers.
When we open our hearts and give our lives to Christ,
   God's forgiveness is truly ours.
In the name of Christ, we are forgiven!

Passing the Peace of Christ (Philippians 2)
Make the joy of God's love and forgiveness complete:
share with one another the love
that Christ shares with us.

Response to the Word (Matthew 21)
What do you think?
When God calls, do you say yes or no?
When Christ leads, do you stay or go?
Let us reflect silently on the answers
to these questions.
(Time of silence or quiet music may follow.)
May we look, not to our own interests,
but to the interests of others.
   May we respond,
   not with the values of this world,
   but with the mind of Christ.
Having the same love, we will be and become
children of compassion and sympathy.
   Sharing in the same Spirit,
   we will live as servants of God.

THANKSGIVING AND COMMUNION

Invitation to the Offering (Philippians 2)
Let the mind of Christ lead us to share generously and
compassionately, not only in this morning's offering but
also in everything we do and everything we say.

*Offering Prayer (Exodus 17, Psalm 78, Philippians 2,
Matthew 21)*
Compassionate Christ,
   transform these offerings with your Spirit,
   that they may accomplish your work in the world.
To the thirsty and hungry,
   may these gifts bring water and food.
To the oppressed and the forgotten,
   may these gifts bring justice and hope.

To the sinful and the selfish,
may these gifts bring grace and new beginnings.
May we, likewise, be your humble servants,
accomplishing your work in this world.

Invitation to Communion (Exodus 17, Psalm 78)

This is the table of grace.
In Holy Communion, manna in the wilderness
becomes the bread of life;
water from a rock
becomes the living stream of Christ's grace;
the promised land comes to us,
that we might know Christ
in the breaking of the bread
and the sharing of the cup.
Come to the table of grace.
Drink of the promise of God.
Feed on the law of love,
and your cup will be filled with a living water
that never ends.

SENDING FORTH

Benediction (Philippians 2, Matthew 21)

May we go forth with the mind of Christ
and the love of God
to serve in the vineyard of life!

CONTEMPORARY OPTIONS

Gathering Words (Philippians 2)

Come, now is the time to worship,
to gather and to praise.
We gather to give glory to God!
Come, now is the time to worship,
to sing and to pray.
We gather to give glory to God!
(This litany can easily lead into the song "Come, Now Is the
Time to Worship.")

Praise Sentences (Psalm 78, Philippians 2)

Tell of God's works! Think on God's deeds!
Give glory and praise to God!
Give glory and praise to God!

OCTOBER 2, 2011

Sixteenth Sunday after Pentecost
World Communion Sunday
Bill Hoppe

COLOR

Green

SCRIPTURE READINGS

Exodus 20:1-4, 7-9, 12-20; Psalm 19; Philippians 3:4b-14;
Matthew 21:33-46

THEME IDEAS

The law of God, and what it means to truly uphold this law,
is the focus of today's readings. From the time that the
Lord's commandments are given to Moses and the people
of Israel, the law is both a blessing to those who understand
its message and a curse to those who can read it only as a set
of rigid, unbending rules. Paul's letter to the Philippians reveals and clarifies the meaning of righteousness, and Jesus
makes it quite clear that the kingdom of heaven belongs to
those who understand God's word to be a living, breathing
entity: the love story of the Creator for all of creation.

INVITATION AND GATHERING

Call to Worship (Exodus 20)
O Lord, you are God.
There is no other God but you.

We renounce all that we have allowed
to come between us.
O Lord, we worship you.
We praise and honor your name.
We worship you on this, your holy day.
For your love, for your word,
for all that you have given:
O Lord, we thank you and praise you.
We love you.

Opening Prayer (Psalm 19)
Almighty God,
your word bursts forth into our lives
like a glorious sunrise.
You speak, and our hearts rejoice.
You command, and our eyes are opened.
The sound of your voice brings revival to our souls.
Your words are purer than the finest gold.
True and righteous one, living Word,
light our way.
As we listen to your Spirit,
may the words of our mouths
and the thoughts of our hearts
be accepted in your sight, O Lord,
our strength and our redeemer. Amen.

PROCLAMATION AND RESPONSE

Prayer of Confession (Philippians 3)
No matter how righteous
we imagine ourselves to be, Lord,
your perfect word reveals our imperfections
all too clearly.
No matter how hard we strive
to fulfill the requirements of your law,
we always fall short.
We have forgotten that righteousness and perfection
come not from rules and regulations
but from faith.

We have ignored the truth that your righteousness
   comes from faith.
Open our eyes to see that all we have accomplished
   is nothing compared to knowing Christ
      as our Lord.
Let us count everything as loss,
   that we might gain heaven
   and be found blameless in Christ.
In the name of the Savior we pray. Amen.

Words of Assurance (Philippians 3)
Take heart; have faith. The goal is in sight.
Press on to take hold of it,
   as Christ has taken hold of us.
Have no fear; leave the past behind.
Reach out for what lies ahead, for the prize,
   for the life to be found in Christ Jesus.

Response to the Word (Matthew 21)
The weight of your words, your laws,
   your commandments and decrees
      can become an impossible burden, Lord,
      if we allow them to overwhelm and crush us.
Yet they were meant to be life-giving,
   vital and alive—
      the foundation for our lives,
      the chief cornerstone of your church,
      the living temple of God.
Loving God, this is your handiwork.
How amazing and wonderful it is!

THANKSGIVING AND COMMUNION

Offering Prayer (Psalm 19, Philippians 3)
Lord of grace and forgiveness,
   you who gave everything
      and spared nothing
         to make us your own,
         we offer back to you
            what you have so freely given to us.

Let all that we say and do,
all that we think and plan and consider,
be pleasing to you, blessed Creator,
Provider, and Savior,
in whose name we pray. Amen.

SENDING FORTH

Benediction (Psalm 19, Matthew 21)
Hear the voice of the Creator, the mighty God,
the One who built the vault of heaven,
who set the sun on its blazing course
through the skies!
Hear the words of life,
declared not by speech or language or voice
but written on the heart!
Go forth in the name of the living Word,
the One whose words bring forth
the fruit of the kingdom in your own lives! Amen.

CONTEMPORARY OPTIONS

Gathering Words (Psalm 19)
The heavens shout out the glory of God!
The universe declares God's work!
We hear no voice or speech.
Yet the word is heard in all the earth!
The word of the Lord reaches to the end of the world!
Thanks and praise be to our God!

Praise Sentences (Psalm 19)
The word of the Lord is perfect!
God's word revives the soul!
The decrees of God never fail!
Our hearts rejoice!
The word of God shines clear!
Our eyes are enlightened!
The word of the Lord endures forever!
Blessed be God's holy name!

OCTOBER 9, 2011

Seventeenth Sunday after Pentecost
Mary J. Scifres

COLOR

Green

SCRIPTURE READINGS

Exodus 32:1-14; Psalm 106:6, 19-23; Philippians 4:1-9; Matthew 22:1-14

THEME IDEAS

Missed opportunities abound in the Exodus story and in Jesus' parable. The Hebrew people miss the opportunity to worship Yahweh in spirit and truth. Invited guests miss the opportunity to celebrate God's realm in the form of a wedding banquet. Another guest misses the opportunity to clothe himself in the dress of the kingdom. Could the wedding robe be symbolic of truly glorifying God (as the Hebrew people neglected to do), clothing oneself in constant rejoicing and prayer (as Philippians recommends), or perhaps clothing oneself in love and grace (as Colossians suggests)? When we give God glory, when we show our constant gratitude, and when we live our gratitude by focusing on honorable things worthy of praise, we embrace the opportunity to celebrate God's realm and even bring God's realm into being on this earth.

INVITATION AND GATHERING

Call to Worship (Exodus 32, Psalm 106, Philippians 4)
Come, let us put God in the center of our lives!
We rejoice in God's steadfast love!
Come, let our gentleness be a reflection of God's love.
We give thanks for Christ's enduring grace!
Come, let us lay down our burdens and worries.
We offer our needs to God in prayer.
Come, let us focus on what is honorable and true.
With hope, we turn now to God's guiding word.

Opening Prayer (Psalm 106, Philippians 4)
Most Holy God,
we come into worship
with thanksgiving and praise,
but we also come before you
with worries and doubts.
As we lay these burdens down,
fill us with your Spirit
and bless us with peace and joy.
Keep our minds in Christ Jesus,
that we may remain focused
on issues of justice and righteousness,
love and grace.
In Christ's name, we pray. Amen.

PROCLAMATION AND RESPONSE

Prayer of Confession (Exodus 32, Philippians 4)
Most Holy God,
we have made gods out of gold and clay;
we have allowed worries and doubts
to cloud our vision and faith.
Do not think on these things, gracious God.
Find in us all that is honorable and true,
commendable and excellent.

Shine in our lives,
    that we may reflect the just and righteous parts
      of ourselves.
Forgive us when we reflect false gods or sinful values.
Guide us back into your holy presence
    and transform us with your grace,
    that we may be the gentle and just people
      you would have us be and become.

Words of Assurance (Philippians 4)
The peace of God, which surpasses all understanding,
    is ours through Christ Jesus.
In Christ, we are forgiven indeed!

Passing the Peace of Christ (Philippians 4)
Let us show one another signs of God's peace,
the peace beyond all understanding
that is yours and mine to share.
The amazing peace of God be with you.
    And also with you.

Preparation to Hear the Word (Philippians 4)
Beloved friends, let us think now on whatever is honorable and true, on what is just and pure, on all that is pleasing and commendable, excellent and worthy of praise.

Response to the Word (Philippians 4, Matthew 22)
Holy One,
    clothe us in your compassion and love.
Dress us in your justice and righteousness.
Transform us to be people of your realm,
    living the words we so often pray:
      "Your kingdom come. Your will be done,
        on earth as it is in heaven."

THANKSGIVING AND COMMUNION

Invitation to the Offering (Exodus 32)
Come, lay your gifts before God. Let God's refining fire transform our gold and silver into justice and righteousness for a world in desperate need.

Offering Prayer (Psalm 106, Philippians 4, Matthew 22)
> God of steadfast love,
>> we thank you for the abundant gifts in our lives:
>>> love and grace, clothing and belongings,
>>> friends and family.
>
> We thank you for the steadfast signs
>> of your loving presence in our world:
>>> wondrous works and awesome deeds.
>
> We come before you with our offerings,
>> rejoicing in this opportunity
>>> to help bring your realm to this earth.

SENDING FORTH

Benediction (Philippians 4)
> May the peace of God,
>> which surpasses all understanding,
>> keep your hearts and minds in Christ Jesus
>> this day and forevermore. Amen.

CONTEMPORARY OPTIONS

Gathering Words (Exodus 32, Psalm 106, Philippians 4, Matthew 22)
> Many are called, but few are chosen.
> How shall we come before our God?
> Shall we come focused on worries
>> and busy schedules,
>>> striving for wealth and power?
> Or shall we come open to joy,
>> prepared to listen and live our lives
>>> with justice and love?
> Many are called, but few are chosen.
> How shall we come before our God?

Praise Sentences (Philippians 4)
> Rejoice in God always! Again I say rejoice!
> **Rejoice in God always! Again I say rejoice!**

Praise Sentences (Psalm 106)

For steadfast love that endures forever,
praise Christ Jesus above!
Praise Christ Jesus above!

OCTOBER 16, 2011

Eighteenth Sunday after Pentecost

Roberta J. Egli

COLOR

Green

SCRIPTURE READINGS

Exodus 33:12-23; Psalm 99; 1 Thessalonians 1:1-10; Matthew 22:15-22

THEME IDEAS

We strive to have the ways of God revealed in concrete and tangible ways. Yet, with our limitations, we fail to recognize that God is revealed through all things. Moses needs assurance that God will not leave him alone and pleads to see God's face so that he can trust God's presence at all times. The psalmist proclaims that God is revealed in the quaking of the earth, the pillars of clouds, and in the high mountains. All of the earth belongs to God, revealing God's goodness and love of justice. In response, we are called to break into glorious songs of praise. In 1 Thessalonians, God's love is revealed through the life, death, and resurrection of Jesus Christ. Through the power of the Spirit, we respond to Christ by being steadfast in hope, as we labor in love, revealing Christ's love to all people. In Matthew, Jesus reveals that the ways of God are not narrow but, rather, broad and all-encompassing.

INVITATION AND GATHERING

Call to Worship (Exodus 33, Psalm 99)
    As we gather to worship you, Holy One,
      show us your presence, O God.
    As we join to pray at your footstool, Exalted One,
      show us your ways, O God.
    As we unite our voices to praise you, Lover of Justice,
      show us your glory, O God.
    As we tremble in the cleft of the rock,
    silently awaiting you, Merciful One,
      show us your goodness, O God.
    Let the earth shake in your praise, Most High!
      We extol your great and awesome name,
      ever-present God!

Opening Prayer (Exodus 33, 1 Thessalonians 1,
Matthew 22)
    Living God,
      move among us and awaken us
        to your loving presence.
    When we lose our way
      and put our confidence in our possessions
        and our wisdom,
        call us back to you.
    Remind us that our very identity
      is dependent on your abiding mercy.
    Show us how to walk with steadfast faithfulness,
      following the path of justice and goodness
        in our daily lives.
    May our days be filled with joy and hope
      as we share the good news of abundant life
        that comes from following Jesus Christ.
    In the power of the Holy Spirit, we pray. Amen.

PROCLAMATION AND RESPONSE

Prayer of Confession (Exodus 33, Matthew 22)
    God of mercy,
      we place our trust in tangible things—

things we can see and touch—
and question whether you are really there.
Forgive us, Holy One,
when we fail to recognize
that you are always nearby,
patiently waiting for us to recognize
your presence and your glory.
Help us when we lose our way,
and forgive us when we forget
to whom we truly belong.
Lover of justice,
open our eyes to see you;
open our ears to hear you;
open our hearts to love you;
and open our hands to serve you.

Words of Assurance (Exodus 33:14, Psalm 99)

When we cry to God, looking for favor in God's sight,
God answers: "My presence will go with you,
and I will give you rest."
In the power of the Spirit and in the name of Jesus,
we are forgiven!
We will rest in God's mercy!

Passing the Peace of Christ (1 Thessalonians 1)

Brothers and sisters, Christ is present in the eyes of a
stranger. As beloved children of God, Christ is recognized
as we touch one another. Turn to one another, seeing and
touching Christ as we share the peace of Christ.

THANKSGIVING AND COMMUNION

Invitation to the Offering (Matthew 22)

Christ is made known in the answer to a difficult question
meant to entrap him. Christ calls us to give to God the
things that belong to God, and to give to the emperor
those things that do not originate in the goodness of God's
love. We hear Christ's words this day as we strive to be

stewards of God's great mercy. Let us give generously as we too remember that our very selves belong to God.

Offering Prayer (Psalm 99, Matthew 22)
God, source of all that is,
> lover of justice and source of equity,
> help us live boldly and truthfully
>> as we seek to follow your ways.
Embolden us to share with others the gift of grace
> that you have so abundantly given us.
Receive and bless these gifts
> that we return to you now.
In the name of the One who gives us life, we pray. Amen.

SENDING FORTH

Benediction (1 Thessalonians 1)
Go from this place with the confidence
that you are God's beloved children.
> **We go, to labor in love with all we meet.**
Go out into the world with steadfast hope
and joyous trust.
> **We go, remembering our faithful God**
> **who goes before us.**
In God's love, the Spirit's power,
and the peace of Christ, go now in peace.

CONTEMPORARY OPTIONS

Gathering Words (Psalm 99, 1 Thessalonians 1)
Come and give thanks to God,
constantly remembering God's faithfulness.
> **The Lord our God is holy!**
> **Praise the name of the Lord.**
Come before God with abiding faith
and steadfast hope.
> **The Lord our God is holy!**
> **Praise the name of the Lord.**

Come hear the powerful message
of good news in Christ.
The Lord our God is holy!
Praise the name of the Lord.

Praise Sentences (Psalm 99)
The Lord is the great King!
Praise God's holy name!
The Lord is the great King!
Praise God's holy name.

OCTOBER 23, 2011

Nineteenth Sunday after Pentecost
Mary J. Scifres

COLOR

Green

SCRIPTURE READINGS

Deuteronomy 34:1-12; Psalm 90:1-6, 13-17;
1 Thessalonians 2:1-8; Matthew 22:34-46

THEME IDEAS

There is danger in loving God and others as completely
as scripture suggests. Such love guides Moses to lead his
sister and brother Hebrews through the wilderness, year
after year; yet Moses himself never reaches the promised
land. Such love guides early church leaders like Paul,
Peter, and Timothy to plant and visit new Christian com-
munities—even when they fight among themselves and
against their leaders. Such love guides Jesus to speak the
truth, to live by God's teachings, to include the most re-
viled outcasts—even when those actions lead to his death
on a cross. Such love has been God's love for humanity
since the beginning of time, through all generations, and
for all ages to come. God's love is ours from everlasting to
everlasting, and God's words to us remain the same: love
with all your heart, and with all your soul, and with all
your mind. Such love brings great risk, but such love is
the only true path to experiencing God's love completely.

INVITATION AND GATHERING

Call to Worship (Psalm 90, Matthew 22)
God welcomes us this day with steadfast love
to satisfy our deepest longings.
Praise God who has been our dwelling place
in every generation.
Before the mountains were formed
and we were still dust, God loved us into being.
Praise God who created us and renews us still.
May God's favor and grace guide us
on paths of love and peace.
We rejoice with gladness this day!

—Or—

Call to Worship (Matthew 22)
Love the Lord your God.
We come with love and hope!
Love your neighbors too.
We come with loving hearts.
Love even yourself.
We come in humble trust.
Love and you will live.
We come to worship God,
that love might live in us.

Opening Prayer (Matthew 22)
God of ages past and days to come,
be with us this day.
Shower us with your love and truth.
Open our hearts and minds
to truly love as you love us
and as you call us to love.
Grant us the courage to ask
the questions that frighten us,
that we may courageously live and grow
as your disciples on this earth.
With the confidence of Christ's grace in our lives,
we pray. Amen.

PROCLAMATION AND RESPONSE

Prayer of Confession (Psalm 90, Matthew 22)

God of steadfast love,
turn away your anger and frustration:
when we fall short in your eyes,
when we forget to love,
when we are afraid to love,
when we neglect to love.
Forgive us and transform us
with your amazing grace.
Fill us with your love so completely
that our lives may overflow with love—
in heart, mind, and soul. Amen.

—Or—

Prayer of Confession (Deuteronomy 34, Psalm 90, Matthew 22)

Everlasting God,
you have been our dwelling place
in each generation.
Since the creation of the world,
you have nurtured us with your love.
And yet we shamefully acknowledge
that we do not always share your love with others.
We are selective about who we choose as neighbors:
those who are clean,
those who look like us,
those who talk right,
those who seem safe.
Loving God,
teach us to love you more fully.
For in loving you,
our lives show love to those we see as "other,"
even as your love encompasses all your creation,
in all generations.
We pray in the name of your greatest gift of love,
Jesus Christ. Amen.
(Laura Jaquith Bartlett)

Words of Assurance (Psalm 90)

God's compassion is sufficient for all our needs.
In the name of Christ, you are forgiven!
In the name of Christ, you are forgiven!

Passing the Peace of Christ (Matthew 22)

Love God with all your heart, with all your soul, and with all your mind. Love your neighbor as yourself. Simple words. Profound challenges. Let us begin by sharing signs of love and peace with one another.

Response to the Word (Matthew 22)

What must we do to live God's law?
Love the Lord your God.
How much must we love?
With all your heart, with all your soul,
and with all your mind.
Whom else must we love?
Our neighbors, both near and far.
Even neighbors we know and neighbors we fear?
Friends and enemies, strangers and family.
How can we love so completely?
Because Christ first loved us.
Must I love myself too?
Even ourselves must we love.
May it be so.
May it be so.

THANKSGIVING AND COMMUNION

Invitation to the Offering (Psalm 90, Matthew 22)

From everlasting to everlasting, God has cared for us. Let us show our love and concern for others as we give of ourselves in this time of offering.

Offering Prayer (Psalm 90, Matthew 22)

God of abundant love,
multiply these gifts
to become gifts of abundant love
for a world in need.
In the name of Christ who first loved us, we pray.

SENDING FORTH

Benediction (Matthew 22)

Go forth in the knowledge and love of God.
We go, confident in God's steadfast love.
Go into the world, loving without limits,
caring without boundaries.
We journey forth to fulfill God's law of love.

CONTEMPORARY OPTIONS

Gathering Words (Matthew 22)

(The following thoughts may be printed for contemplation or spoken alone by a solo voice. Bolded phrases also provide the option of a responsive litany.)

Love, love, love.
The gospel in a word is love.
So say the words of an old camp song.
Simple song, simple words.
The gospel in a word is love.
Jesus said it this way.
All the law and the commandments
hang on two great commands:
Love God with all your heart, soul, and mind;
love your neighbor as yourself.
Love, love, love.
The challenge in a word is love.
So says a life of trying to live these commands.
Challenging life, challenging words.
Jesus' life in a word is love.

Praise Sentences (Psalm 90, Matthew 22)

Love God with all your heart.
We rejoice in God's steadfast love!
Love God with all your soul.
We rejoice in God's steadfast love!
Love God with all your mind.
We rejoice in God's steadfast love!

OCTOBER 30, 2011

Twentieth Sunday after Pentecost
Reformation Sunday

Mary J. Scifres

COLOR
Green

SCRIPTURE READINGS
Joshua 3:7-17; Psalm 107:1-7, 33-37;
1 Thessalonians 2:9-13; Matthew 23:1-12

THEME IDEAS
Humility and thanksgiving emerge as prominent themes in today's scriptures. In ancient days, the priests of Israel humbled themselves to walk first into the chilly waters of the Jordan. Risking more than wet robes, they led the faithful across what became dry land—but only after the priests' feet had touched the muddy water. The scribes and Pharisees of Jesus' day were called to a similar level of courageous leadership and faithful servanthood. But when they did not practice what they preached, Jesus rebuked them and called for a return to humble servanthood. From ages past to modern times, a life of gratitude can return us to the humble remembrance of our dependence on God, on one another, and on God's good earth. Whether preparing for fall festivals, Halloween celebrations, calls of stewardship, or even an early celebration of

the season of thanksgiving, today's scriptures invite us to give thanks for saving miracles, abundant harvests, hard work, caring leaders, and a loving God who guides and nurtures us through all of life's circumstances.

INVITATION AND GATHERING

Call to Worship (Joshua 3, Psalm 107)

Draw near and hear the words of God.
We gather to listen and pray.
Draw near with humble hearts and open minds.
We hunger and thirst for God.
Draw near to walk this journey of faith.
We follow in the footsteps of Christ.
Draw near and drink deep of the marrow of life.
We come to worship the Lord our God.

Opening Prayer (Joshua 3, Psalm 107, Matthew 23)

God of earth and heaven,
  we hunger and thirst
    for your presence in our lives
      and in our world.
Nurture us with your truth this day,
  and strengthen us with your word.
May your love be the foundation
  upon which we stand.
May your teachings be the starting block
  from which we run the marathon of faithful living.
Guide us this day and all days,
  that we may be a people who serve and love
    as you love and care for us.

PROCLAMATION AND RESPONSE

Prayer of Confession (Joshua 3, Matthew 23)

Rabbi, Father, Teacher, Mother, Gracious God,
  we come to you with humble hearts.
You see us at our best and at our worst.

You know when we have grabbed the seats of honor,
or when we have assumed that the earth's gifts
are ours for the taking.
You know when we have been judgmental
rather than encouraging.
And you know when we have enjoyed power
rather than choosing the role of the servant.
When we exalt ourselves, forgive us.
(A time of silence may follow.)

Rabbi, Father, Teacher, Mother, Gracious God,
we come to you with humble hearts.
Hear our prayers and guide us through the waters
onto the dry ground of humble servanthood—
the promised land of faith. Amen.

Words of Assurance (Joshua 3)
Draw near, brothers and sisters,
and know that we are led as miraculously
as those first followers of God.
By Christ's grace, we are led forth into freedom—
freedom to serve and to live,
for God forgives us again
and calls us to be a people of faith and hope.

Passing the Peace of Christ (Psalm 107)
From the east and the west, the north and the south, the
people of God have gathered. From strength and weakness, from abundance and hunger, the people of God have
gathered. Thanks be to God for the steadfast love that welcomes us here! Let us share this miraculous community
as we greet one another in the name of Christ.

Response to the Word (Joshua 3, Psalm 107, Matthew 23)
We have drawn near and heard the words of God.
We give thanks and praise, for God is good.
God's love endures forever!

God holds back the waters that hinder our way.
We give thanks and praise, for God is good.
God's love endures forever!
God leads us to faith and nurtures our hope.
We give thanks and praise, for God is good.
God's love endures forever!
God calls us to serve, to care, and to love.
We give thanks and praise, for God is good.
God's love endures forever!

THANKSGIVING AND COMMUNION

Invitation to the Offering (Psalm 107, Matthew 23)

As God turns deserts into pools of water, and gives fruitful fields for the hungry to live, so now God invites us to turn parched lands into springs of water, and barren lands into fruitful vineyards with our gifts and offerings. Let us share generously, in humble servanthood and faithful gratitude, that others may live in abundance and hope.

Offering Prayer (Psalm 107)

Lord of all the earth,
we thank you for your abundant gifts:
for water that refreshes,
fields that nourish,
and fruit that sweetens life.
As we share the fruits of our labor with your world,
let them become abundant gifts
to those who need refreshment, nourishment,
and sweet surprises.
In gratitude, we pray. Amen.

SENDING FORTH

Benediction (Joshua 3, Matthew 23)

With thanks and praise, we have drawn near
and heard your teachings.
We have heard God's challenging word.
With love and grace, Christ has drawn near to us.
We go forth with Christ's love in our hearts.

In humility and gratitude, we are called to serve.
We will shower God's world with love.

CONTEMPORARY OPTIONS

Gathering Words (Joshua 3, Psalm 107, Matthew 23)
God's love is forever. Christ's grace is near.
We gather to celebrate this truth.
God's guidance is ours. Christ's teachings are clear.
We gather to celebrate this truth.
God calls us to praise. Christ calls us to serve.
We gather to celebrate this truth.
Draw near, my friends. Hear the word.
We gather to celebrate God's truth!

Praise Sentences (Psalm 107)
Give thanks and praise, for God is good!
Christ's steadfast love endures forever!
Give thanks and praise, for God is good!
Christ's steadfast love endures forever!

NOVEMBER 1, 2011

All Saints Day
Beryl A. Ingram

COLOR
White

SCRIPTURE READINGS
Revelation 7:9-17; 1 John 3:1-3; Psalm 34:1-10, 22;
Matthew 5:1-12

THEME IDEAS
All Saints Day conjures images of that great cloud of witnesses gathered so near to us that it creates palpable en-
ergy. Revelation pictures saints from every place and
time—everyone is there—singing in the presence of God.
First John gives us a glimpse of what is in store for us as
we go on to perfection, filled increasingly with God.
Psalm 34 invites us to praise God, whose goodness is beyond our comprehension. The Beatitudes (or BE-Atti-
tudes) in Matthew affirm those who are marginalized by
humility, sorrow, care-giving, longing for right relationships with God and neighbor, and even living the gospel
of Jesus Christ, for what appears weak or impoverished to
the world actually touches the heart of God. As we allow
God to direct more and more of our life choices, we grow
in holiness as we are filled with love.

INVITATION AND GATHERING

Call to Worship (Revelation 7)
As we gather, we remember that we are not alone!
We gather with the saints,
who live in the presence of God,
singing praises to the God of our salvation.
From every nation, race, clan, and culture,
God's people gather to worship
the One-Who-Is-without-Peer!
To God and to the Lamb, all honor, glory,
wisdom, thanksgiving, strength, and power.
Blessed be God, now and forever! Amen!
Amen!

—Or—

Call to Worship (Psalm 34)
Let us bless God every chance we get.
We bless the God of our salvation!
Magnify the Lord.
We lift up God's name in praise!
O taste and see that God is good.
Those who make their home in God
are filled with joy.
Magnify the Lord.
Lift God's name in praise!

Opening Prayer (Psalm 34, Matthew 5)
Blessed are you, God of our salvation.
As we turn to you in prayer,
be with us and reveal to us your ways
From your self-revelation in Jesus,
teach us how to live in ways that honor you:
by humbling ourselves;
by being content with what we have
rather than striving for more;
by caring and cooperating,
rather than competing in unhealthy ways.

Teach us, giver of all goodness,
   to be strong in your strength
      for the sake of the gospel.
Help us honor your prodigal grace,
   by living as doers of peace
      in this world you love. Amen.

PROCLAMATION AND RESPONSE

Prayer of Confession (All Saints)
Holy God, we so often fail to remember
how profoundly you love us.
   You bless us even when we are at our wit's end.
You created us, and you love us as we are,
even as you inspire our desire to be better
through your Holy Spirit.
   Forgive us when we fail to remember
   that we are the body of Christ,
   saints-in-process.
Empower us to begin anew,
encouraged by the stories of those
who live in your eternal presence.
   In the name of Jesus,
   and for the sake of the gospel,
   we pray. Amen.

Words of Assurance
Beloved, we are the children of God.
Don't fear failure.
It is endemic to our human nature.
Learn from your mistakes,
   and cherish the forgiving grace of God.
Give thanks for all you are, and go forward in faith,
   knowing that God is faithful.

Response to the Word (Matthew 5)
You are blest when your last option fails.
   For without the gift of failure,
   our vision will not clear to see new possibilities;

our eyes will not be able to see the God
who is there for us in new, life-giving ways.
You are blest when you care for others
and when you are kind and compassionate.
As we are to others, God will be to us.
You are blest when your heart is filled with God.
As others see God in us,
we will see God everywhere.
You are blest when you choose nonviolence
as your response of choice.
As we seek good for others,
rather than harm for them,
others will recognize the God-within-us.
You are blest when you live for God
and people despise you and turn on you
for your kingdom choices.
When we live for God,
despite the persecution it brings,
we find ourselves in holy company—
saints and prophets and all who love God.
We find ourselves with Jesus
standing next to us, smiling.

THANKSGIVING AND COMMUNION

Offering Prayer (Revelation 7)

Holy God,
> we thank you for the great cloud of witnesses
> > that surrounds us as we worship.
Their diversity reminds us of your infinite grace
> to all your creatures.
Thank you for the vision of a world at peace:
> paradise restored, where no one hungers,
> > no one thirsts, and no one is wanting
> > in any way.
You guide us to the source of living water
> and invite us to drink deeply of your love.

Your magnificent generosity
   evokes our deepest thanks.
And so receive these offerings,
   that we may join that great cloud of witnesses
      as we share our gifts with others. Amen.

SENDING FORTH

Benediction (Psalm 34)
   We are renewed and filled with the sweetness of God.
   Go forth to bless the world with joy
      in the Spirit of God's redemptive love
      and sustaining peace. Amen.

CONTEMPORARY OPTIONS

Call to Worship (Revelation 7:16-17)
   All right!
      All right!
   What do we offer to God today?
      Blessing, glory, wisdom, thanksgiving, honor,
      power, and strength!
   All this to our God?
      Yes, to our God, forever and ever and ever!
   All right!
      All right!

—Or—

Call to Worship (1 John 3)
   We are God's children, here, now, today!
      Who will we be tomorrow?
   We are God's children!
      When Christ comes again we will see and know
      exactly who God is calling us to be.
   We will see God face to face.
      We will understand the mystery of love!

Praise Sentences (Psalm 34, 1 John 3)
Bless God all the time.
Praise God!
We are children of the living God!
Praise God!
Praise God!
Praise God!

NOVEMBER 6, 2011

Twenty-first Sunday after Pentecost
Mary J. Scifres

COLOR
Green

SCRIPTURE READINGS
Joshua 24:1-3a, 14-25; Psalm 78:1-7;
1 Thessalonians 4:13-18; Matthew 25:1-13

THEME IDEAS
In this season, formerly known as kingdomtide, we encounter some of the most challenging words of scripture.
Choosing to lead a life of faith brings both challenge and
consequence. The challenge to declare our faith is one sort
of challenge—a challenge faced by the tribes of Israel after
many years of traveling among foreign peoples and foreign beliefs. But the challenge to constantly be alert and
prepared, vividly portrayed in Matthew 25, is perhaps the
greater struggle. In either case, scripture warns us that the
failure to meet the challenge can bring dire consequences.
We see this in the analogy to marriage. Many people
struggle to make the commitment of marriage. But even
after this commitment is finally reached, building and
maintaining a marriage is a lifelong task and challenge.
With Joshua's reference to family and Jesus' reference to
brides and bridegrooms, there are rich images available
to examine the challenges of faith and commitment at

many different levels today—and the consequences of our abilities (or inabilities) to meet these challenges.

INVITATION AND GATHERING

Call to Worship (Joshua 24, Psalm 78)
> Choose this day to sing with joy.
> **We give thanks and praise to God!**
> Choose this day to love and serve.
> **We rejoice in Christ's call in our lives!**
> Choose this day to worship God.
> **We gather to worship and pray.**

Opening Prayer or Words of Reflection
(Psalm 78, Matthew 25)
> We gather this day to listen for God's ancient truths,
> stories of wisdom passed down through the ages.
> We gather this day to listen for Christ's ongoing call,
> challenging words shared from generation
> to generation.
> We gather this day to listen for the Spirit's movement,
> the wind of change that pushes us
> into new dimensions of truth and discipleship.
> Speak to us, O God,
> that we may hear your truth,
> both ancient and new.

PROCLAMATION AND RESPONSE

Prayer of Confession (Joshua 24, Psalm 78,
Matthew 25)
> Holy One,
> we gather this day with the knowledge
> that our choice to serve you
> carries challenges each and every day.
> Forgive us when we fail to meet those challenges.
> When we are unprepared for what we face,
> strengthen us with new resolve
> and better abilities to move forward in faith.

When we stray onto paths of danger and betrayal,
    lead us back to your path of truth and love.
Let your words ring true in our lives,
    that we may love and serve you—
        loving and serving your world
            in all that we say and in all that we do.
In hope and trust, we pray. Amen.

—Or—

Prayer of Confession (Matthew 25:1-13)

Forgive us, Christ Jesus,
    when we put you last in our lives.
Forgive us when we let our lamps burn out.
When we run too fast,
    when we work too hard,
    when we sleep too long,
    when we stretch ourselves too thin;
        forgive us and renew us.
Let your Spirit flow through our lives,
    filling our lamps,
    that we might shine for others in need.
In Christ's name we pray. Amen.

Words of Assurance (Matthew 25)

Keep awake!
But even when you sleep,
    know that God is our keeper,
    Christ is our savior,
    and the Spirit is always with us.
Rise in hope and joy, my friends.
In the name of Christ, we are forgiven
    and reconciled to God.

Passing the Peace of Christ (Joshua 24, Matthew 25)

As forgiven and reconciled children of God, let us be reconciled to one another. Share your oil, trim one another's lamps, serve one another even as we serve God. Come! Let us share signs of love and reconciliation as we pass the peace of Christ.

*Preparation for or Response to the Word
(Joshua 24, Psalm 78, Matthew 25)*
Prepared or unprepared, we face God's challenges
each and every day.
**Setting our hope in God,
we trust that Christ will lead the way.**
Choosing or not choosing, our actions dictate
who we are, each and every day.
**Setting our hope in God,
we trust that Christ will lead the way.**
God's glorious deeds and Christ's miraculous grace
make possible this path of faith and love.
**Setting our hope in God,
we know that Christ will lead the way.**

THANKSGIVING AND COMMUNION

Invitation to the Offering (Matthew 25)
Ten bridesmaids were given lamps with oil. Some had additional oil, others did not. Let us give out of the abundance that we have been given. Whether our lamps are filled to the brim or barely burning, we are called to share so that others may see Christ's light.

Offering Prayer (Psalm 78, Matthew 25)
As we celebrate the many wonders in our lives,
we give you thanks and praise, O God.
Transform these offerings
into gifts of wonder and glorious deeds,
that all may see the light of your love,
leading us to abundant life.

SENDING FORTH

Benediction (Matthew 25)
Keep awake, for darkness is all around!
May our hearts shine with God's love.
Keep awake, for the world is in constant need!
**May we see and respond
where Christ calls us to serve.**

CONTEMPORARY OPTIONS

Gathering Words (Matthew 25)

Ten bridesmaids went forth.
All were prepared for a night of joy.
Ten bridesmaids waited, slowly falling asleep,
    waiting for midnight to come.
Ten bridesmaids awoke at the sound of a shout,
    surprised by the late night hour.
Five bridesmaids went away to buy more oil
    and found themselves left behind.
Where is the joy?
Where is the grace?
Where is the generosity of neighbors and friends?
Are we the unprepared maids?
Are we the self-protective keepers of extra oil?
Are we the demanding bridegroom?
Are we the oil for someone else's lamp?
Or is Christ the oil we desperately seek?
Think on these things. Question and ponder.
For in the challenge of faith,
we are renewed and strengthened to grow.

Praise Sentences (Psalm 78)

O hope in the Lord and tell of Christ's story.
We sing the great deeds of God!
O hope in the Lord and tell of Christ's story.
We sing the great deeds of God!

NOVEMBER 13, 2011

Twenty-second Sunday after Pentecost
Mary J. Scifres

COLOR

Green

SCRIPTURE READINGS

Judges 4:1-7; Psalm 123; 1 Thessalonians 5:1-11;
Matthew 25:14-30

THEME IDEAS

Look! Watch! Be aware! All of today's readings point to a
need for awareness. As we move toward Advent, our
readings begin to focus more directly on preparing for
God's realm and reign upon this earth. All too often, the
Israelites lost that awareness, and judges like Deborah had
to bring them back into "full alert" status. Christians
today too often look for specific times and signs of God's
return, whereas scripture reminds us that we are called to
constantly live in the light and knowledge of Christ's love
and guidance. Matthew's frightening parable offers many
possible lessons, but all remind us that hiding is not a path
toward God's kingdom. Look! Watch! Be aware! As we
watch and prepare, we are called to live as children of
light, allowing God's reign to guide our lives. As we build
one another up, we lay the foundation for God's realm
upon this earth.

INVITATION AND GATHERING

Call to Worship (Psalm 123, 1 Thessalonians 5)
Lift up your eyes and see God's radiant love.
We lift up our hearts in praise.
Lift up your lives and walk in the light.
We lift up our voices in song.
Open your ears to hear Christ's call.
We open our minds to know God's word.

Opening Prayer (1 Thessalonians 5)
As your children of light and life,
we come to you this day, O God,
in worship and praise,
in awareness and hope.
Shine upon us with the radiant light
of your wisdom and guidance.
Keep alive in us the constant awareness
that you are present in our lives and in our world,
creating your realm of love and salvation.
Keep alive in us the enduring hope
that your strength and power
will overcome the sorrow
and sin of this world.
Strengthen our faith and resolve
to stay awake, alert, and serious
about our call to be children of light.

PROCLAMATION AND RESPONSE

Prayer of Confession (1 Thessalonians 5, Matthew 25)
Merciful God,
you know the fears and failures
that prevent us from living as children of light.
When we hide from your call in our lives,
forgive us and strengthen us to move forward
in courage and faith.
When we fall asleep and ignore your teachings,
forgive us and awaken our spirits
to walk in the light of awareness and truth.

Encourage us, gracious God,
   to be children of hope and love,
   even as we encourage one another
   in this same hope and love.
In hope and trust, we pray. Amen.

Words of Assurance (1 Thessalonians 5)
Sisters and brothers, you are all children of light!
Clothed in faith and love, you are God's own children,
   covered with the hope of salvation in Christ Jesus.
Take heart! Wake up!
We are all forgiven and reconciled to God!

Passing the Peace of Christ (1 Thessalonians 5)
As children of light, let us encourage one another and
build one another up. Let us share together signs of peace
and words of love.

Response to the Word (1 Thessalonians 5, Matthew 25)
We know what time it is.
   Time for us to wake up!
We know what time it is.
   Time for us to turn on the light!
We know what time it is.
   Time for us to live in the light!
We know what time it is.
   Time for us to trust God's love!
We know what time it is.
   Time for us to answer Christ's call!
We know what time it is.
   Time for us to wake up!

THANKSGIVING AND COMMUNION

Invitation to the Offering (1 Thessalonians 5, Matthew 25)
For it is as if our God, going on a journey, summoned
Christ's followers and entrusted all of God's earth to
them. We are the trustees of all that God has given us. Let

us share these gifts in faith and trust, in courage and hope,
as signs of light and love.

Offering Prayer (1 Thessalonians 5, Matthew 25)
Loving God,
receive these gifts, both small and large:
gifts hidden,
gifts multiplied,
gifts shared willingly,
gifts shared begrudgingly.
Transform these gifts into signs of light and love.
Transform our living and our giving,
that we may be children of light,
children of faith and hope.
Transform our lives,
that we may be strong and courageous
as followers of Christ. Amen.

SENDING FORTH

Benediction (1 Thessalonians 5)
We have been clothed in faith and love.
We go forth radiant with God's light.
We are covered with the hope of salvation.
We go forth radiant with Christ's love.
We will be blessed as God's children.
**We go forth strengthened by the power
of the Holy Spirit!**

CONTEMPORARY OPTIONS

Gathering Words (1 Thessalonians 5)
Wake up! God's presence has called us here!
We're awake: God's children of light.
Wake up! The world needs our faith and love.
We're awake: God's children of light.
Wake up! Proclaim the saving love of Christ.
We're awake: God's children of light.

Praise Sentences (Psalm 123)
We lift up our eyes and see God's glory!
We lift up our voices in praise!
We lift up our eyes and see God's glory!
We lift up our voices in praise!

NOVEMBER 20, 2011

Christ the King / Reign of Christ
Ken Burton

COLOR
White

SCRIPTURE READINGS
Ezekiel 34:11-16, 20-24; Psalm 100; Ephesians 1:15-23; Matthew 25:31-46

THEME IDEAS
Ezekiel speaks of the shepherd who searches for lost sheep, rescues them from danger, and feeds them from rich pastures. Mathew makes the metaphor personal, as Jesus blesses the "sheep" who feed the hungry and clothe the naked. Truly, this manner of shepherding is an occasion to join the psalmist in making "a joyful noise to the LORD," for we are indeed God's people, the sheep of God's pasture. We, like the early Christians at Ephesus, know the hope to which we have been called and the riches of our glorious inheritance in Christ. Thus it is that we are both broken and whole, at once healer and healed, at the same time shepherd and sheep.

INVITATION AND GATHERING

Call to Worship (Psalm 100)
Make a joyful noise to the Lord.
Worship God with gladness.

Come into God's presence with singing.
We are God's people, the sheep of God's pasture.
Give thanks to the Lord; bless God's holy name,
**for God's steadfast love is present now
and endures forever.**

Opening Prayer (Ezekiel 34, Ephesians 1, Matthew 25)

Tender, comforting Shepherd,
your steadfast love is present in this place
and resides within each of us.
But sometimes it is hard, so very hard,
to open ourselves to your love.
We feel like scattered sheep,
frightened and alone.
Help us know your loving presence
as we live as your gathered community.
Enlighten our hearts,
that we may know the hope
to which we have been called. Amen.

PROCLAMATION AND RESPONSE

Prayer of Confession (Ezekiel 34, Matthew 25)

Holy One,
we are like sheep
that stray from your fold.
We are the perpetually hungry,
ever in spiritual need,
and at times in physical want.
We are the naked,
with wounds exposed and bleeding.
We are the sick,
fevered, chilled, and in pain.
We are the strangers,
separated from others
and even from ourselves.
Hear us now as we confess our brokenness
and our need. Amen.

Words of Assurance (Matthew 25)
Our creator God sees our hunger and gives us food.
Christ, the healer, touches our wounds,
    offering comfort and blessed relief.
The Spirit blows through us, cools our fever,
    and eases our pain.
God sees and touches and heals our wounds.

Passing the Peace of Christ (Matthew 25)
When we were strangers, Christ welcomed us. Let us
share the peace of Christ with friends and strangers with
words of welcome: "The peace of Christ be with you."

Response to the Word (Ephesians 1)
Faithful Comforter,
    we have heard your word of power and blessing.
May it give us a spirit of wisdom,
    that our eyes and hearts may be opened,
    and that we may know the hope
        to which we have been called. Amen.

THANKSGIVING AND COMMUNION

Invitation to the Offering (Matthew 25)
We are shepherd and sheep, wounded and healer. In the
same spirit, we are both giver and receiver. Even as we
have lavishly received, so now may we generously give.

Offering Prayer (Matthew 25)
Holy One,
    you have given us all that we have
    and all that we are.
Through these gifts and in our lives,
    help us be the shepherds and healers and lovers
        that you are calling us to be. Amen.

SENDING FORTH

Benediction (Ezekiel 34, Matthew 25)
Come, you who are blessed!
Inherit all that is prepared for you!

We leave this sacred space
to claim the riches and glorious inheritance
that are ours through Christ.
Go out into the world to share your blessings
with all in need. Amen.

CONTEMPORARY OPTIONS

Gathering Words (Psalm 100, Ephesians 1)
Be here now and give us wisdom!
Give us hope and make us strong!
Let our hearts be filled with riches!
We praise you, God, and sing your song!

Praise Sentences (Psalm 100, Ephesians 1)
God is great and God is cool!
Hang with me, God.
Make me an instrument of your love!
God is great and God is cool!
Hang with me, God.
Make me an instrument of your love!

NOVEMBER 24, 2011

Thanksgiving Day

B. J. Beu

COLOR

White

SCRIPTURE READINGS

Deuteronomy 8:7-18; Psalm 65; 2 Corinthians 9:6-15;
Luke 17:11-19

THEME IDEAS

Thanksgiving is a time to reflect upon our many blessings.
Deuteronomy reminds us that God is the source of all our
blessings and warns us not to take credit for our wealth
and success. The psalmist affirms that God crowns the year
with bounty; Paul urges us to be cheerful givers; and Jesus
challenges us to offer praise to God for all our blessings.

INVITATION AND GATHERING

Call to Worship (Deuteronomy 8, Psalm 65)

Come to the Lord with praise and thanksgiving!
Worship God with gladness!
Come to the Lord with gratitude and joy!
Shower God with praise!
Come to the Lord with grateful hearts!
Love God with humility!
Come! Worship the Lord.

Opening Prayer (Deuteronomy 8, Psalm 65)
Almighty God,
 you have brought us into a land
  flowing with milk and honey;
 you have blessed us with abundant waters
  welling up in pools and springs;
 you have fulfilled your promise,
  giving us all we need,
   that we may share our bounty
    with those who have no bread to eat
    and no place to sleep.
As we celebrate the bounty of your good land,
 remind us that it is by your power alone
  that we prosper.
Give us humble hearts,
 that we may live each day with true gratitude
  for your many blessings. Amen.

PROCLAMATION AND RESPONSE

Prayer of Confession (2 Corinthians 9)
Merciful God,
 we have lost our way in your promised land.
We have taken credit for our success,
 saying:
  "My power and the might of my own hand
   have gotten me this wealth."
We have not always been cheerful givers,
 saying:
  "Why should I share with others
   what is rightfully mine?"
We have lost our way, O God.
Turn our hearts back to you,
 and loosen the chains that bind our hearts,
 that we may share with others
  as generously as you have shared with us. Amen.

Assurance of Pardon (2 Corinthians 9)
We who are lost are given a promise:
we will be enriched in every way
for our great generosity.
God supplies our every need
and blesses us with unsurpassed grace
through forgiveness in Christ Jesus.

Response to the Word (Deuteronomy 8:11, 17-18)
As we celebrate the bounty of our lives, heed the word of
God: "Take care that you do not forget the LORD your God,
by failing to keep [God's] commandments.... Do not say
to yourself, 'My power and the might of my own hand
have gotten me this wealth.' But remember the LORD your
God, for it is [God] who gives you power to get wealth...."
Let us remember who we are, whose we are, and where
our blessings come from.

THANKSGIVING AND COMMUNION

Invitation to the Offering (2 Corinthians 9:6-7)
Ponder these words to the church at Corinth: "The one
who sows sparingly will also reap sparingly, and the one
who sows bountifully will also reap bountifully. Each of
you must give as you have made up your mind, not re-
luctantly or under compulsion, for God loves a cheerful
giver." As God has provided us with every blessing in
abundance, let us share our abundance with those in
need. We who have enough of everything are called to
share abundantly in every good work, that through our
sharing, much may be sown and much may be reaped.

Offering Prayer (Deuteronomy 8, Psalm 65, 2 Corinthians 9)
Bountiful God,
you touch the earth with strength,
bringing forth food for the harvest;
you visit the earth with rain,
watering the ground to sustain our lives;

259

you crown the year with bounty,
    blessing your people with joy and prosperity.
May our offering sow love in the world
    that the harvest may be bountiful. Amen.

SENDING FORTH

Benediction (Deuteronomy 8, Psalm 65, 2 Corinthians 9)
Remember the Lord your God
who crowns the year with bounty.
    We go with thankful hearts
    to sing God's glory.
Remember the Lord your God
who cares for our world.
    We go with grateful hearts
    to share God's abundant love.
Remember the Lord your God
who gives us all we have.
    We go with loving hearts
    to share God's bountiful harvest!

CONTEMPORARY OPTIONS

Gathering Words (Deuteronomy 8)
Praise God for flowing streams!
    Our God is an awesome God!
Praise God for wheat and barley, iron and copper!
    Our God is an awesome God!
Praise God for the commandments that lead to life!
    Our God is an awesome God!
Praise God who provides for us!
    Our God is an awesome God!

Praise Sentences (2 Corinthians 9)
Praise to the One who supplies our every need!
    Praise to the One who supplies our every need!
Praise to the One who leads us into life!
    Praise to the One who leads us into life!

NOVEMBER 27, 2011

First Sunday of Advent
Peter Bankson

COLOR
Purple

SCRIPTURE READINGS
Isaiah 64:1-9; Psalm 80:1-7, 17-19; 1 Corinthians 1:3-9;
Mark 13:24-37

THEME IDEAS
Advent begins with shadows of tension between hunger
and hope. We hunger to know God's presence in our lives,
but we fear that by our thoughts and deeds we've blocked
the coming of the good news in Christ. We know that God
has reason enough to turn away. And yet, when we look
closely, there are signs of hope. Christ is coming, but we
won't know exactly when. We must be ready!

INVITATION AND GATHERING

Call to Worship (1 Corinthians 1)
Come, people of faith, come join your hearts
in worship.
   We hear the invitation
   and hunger to join in the feast.
God is faithful and calls us into the loving presence
of Jesus, who is the Christ.

We come to join with those who watch
and wait and celebrate. Amen.

Opening Prayer (Isaiah 64, Psalm 80, Mark 13)
O Holy God,
    maker of every thought and thing,
    open our hearts this day,
    that we may know your presence
        in this time and place.
Restore us now,
    so we may see the special gift and calling
    that you have for each of us.
Masterful potter of life,
    mold us into the vessels
    you would have us be.
Help us be ready for your promised return,
    when you will be among us and within us
        with new, creative, healing energy. Amen.

PROCLAMATION AND RESPONSE

Prayer of Confession (Isaiah 64)
Patient, everlasting source of life,
    we know that you are present
        with those who gladly do what's right;
    we know that you remember
        those who remember you;
    we know that your judgment is just.
We hunger for the assurance of your love,
    but in our hearts we feel unclean.
We fear that the acts we think so righteous
    are more like filthy bits of cloth,
        unfit to dress a wound or to clothe the naked.
Do not be angry beyond measure,
    O holy and loving champion of the forgotten.
Do not remember our sins forever,
    but embrace us with your love,
    for we are all your people,
        even though we so often forget.

Words of Assurance (Isaiah 64)

Fear not, for our creator is the loving maker
of every thought and thing.
We are the clay; each one of us is being formed
by God's all-loving hand, crafted for a purpose
and cherished as a vessel made for love.
In the name of Jesus, who is the Christ,
you are forgiven.
In the name of Christ, you are forgiven. Amen.

Passing the Peace of Christ (Psalm 80)

The face of God shines brightly on us,
that we might be saved.
The love of God revives us,
that we might call upon God's name.
Seek out the shining face of God in one another
as we share the peace of Christ.
We share the peace of Christ.

Response to the Word (Mark 13)

God of promised new beginnings,
open our hearts to the nourishment of your word,
so we might know that stirring tremble
deep within us;
open our lives to the fresh bud of fruitful service,
so we might grow with mounting hope
as we wait for your advent among us. Amen.

THANKSGIVING AND COMMUNION

Invitation to the Offering (Isaiah 64, Mark 13)

During this late harvest time, when fruit and grain are gathered in and many are preparing for the cold of winter, God invites us to share what we have gathered so others may have enough. The Holy One, the gracious, giving source of comfort, shapes us into vessels of compassion and invites us to give of our bounty so that others may be fed and clothed and healed and loved. Let us be generous and joyful in our giving.

Offering Prayer (Mark 13)

Holy God, triumphant liberating savior of all,
  receive these gifts
    and the hopeful hearts that offer them
      as part of your bountiful harvest.
Strengthen and sustain us
  through our hungers and our fears
    until your unexpected advent.
Help us as we wait
  to know each day
    that we are a part
      of your generous, expectant household,
        the body of Christ. Amen.

Great Thanksgiving

O Holy God, since ancient times
your splendor has filled the world.
  We praise the wonder of your being,
  O wonderful potter of reality!
Loving Christ our savior, we remember
your redeeming presence, even as we wait.
  Christ our savior, we long for your return.
Empowering Holy Spirit, we pray to know
your presence in this time and place.
  Come fill us as we gather now
  to share your presence in the bread and cup.

SENDING FORTH

Benediction (Mark 13)

As we go out to meet a hungry world,
know that God will give us what we need.
  We go forth to make ready as we wait.
The Holy One, whose love turns fear aside,
will show us what to do.
  Keep watch! The risen Christ is on the way!
  Amen.

CONTEMPORARY OPTIONS

Gathering Words (Mark 13)
In times of hunger, keep watch!
> **The Living Christ is on the way!**

In times of hope, rejoice!
> **The Loving Christ is on the way!**

Keep watch!
> **The Risen Christ is on the way!**

Praise Sentences (Psalm 80, 1 Corinthians 1, Mark 13)
Holy God, awaken your might; come and save us.
> **Make your face shine upon us,**
> **that we may be saved!**

The saving grace of Christ fills us with thanksgiving.
> **Make your face shine upon us,**
> **that we may be saved!**

We watch for the coming of Christ.
> **Make your face shine upon us,**
> **that we may be saved!**

DECEMBER 4, 2011

Second Sunday of Advent
Deborah Sokolove

COLOR
Purple

SCRIPTURE READINGS
Isaiah 40:1-11; Psalm 85:1-2, 8-13; 2 Peter 3:8-15a;
Mark 1:1-8

THEME IDEAS
In these readings, we are told to prepare for the day when God will be among us. Isaiah's vision of comfort and rest comes as a promise to all who struggle, while the Gospel message calls us to repentance in expectation that God will be among us very soon. No one knows the exact time or day, but we can depend on God's promises and love.

INVITATION AND GATHERING

Call to Worship (Psalm 85)
Let us hear what God will speak,
for the Holy One speaks peace to the people,
to the faithful, and to all who turn to God in their hearts.
Steadfast love and faithfulness will meet.
Righteousness and peace will embrace.
Faithfulness will spring up from the ground,
and righteousness will look down from the sky.

The Holy One will give what is good,
and we will bring our praise and song.

—Or—

Gathering Words (Isaiah 40)
The world is dark and cold.
We look for signs of your coming.
The world is hungry for righteousness.
We look for signs of your coming.
The world yearns for your love.
We look for signs of your coming.

Opening Prayer (Isaiah 40, Psalm 85, 2 Peter 3)
God of winter and starlight,
    you have promised us your presence:
        to live among us,
        to right all wrongs,
        to bring good things to all who wait
            for your new day.
In these dark days,
    we look for signs of your coming:
        the sounds of children at play,
        the music that fills our hearts
            with anticipation,
        the company of all who serve
            the last and the least.
Make us at home with righteousness,
    that we may be ready to walk
        in your holy ways. Amen.

PROCLAMATION AND RESPONSE

Prayer of Confession (Isaiah 40, Psalm 85)
God of love and kindness,
you have promised to renew our lives,
to be with us in a new heaven and new earth—
a realm where steadfast love and faithfulness
embrace forever.

We are afraid of your promised coming.
We cling to rules we understand:
the rules of privilege and power.
We are afraid of a world of true justice and peace,
afraid that you will change the way
things have always been.
As we wait for you to live among us,
we confess our unwillingness to see
that you have always been here.

Words of Assurance (Isaiah 40, Psalm 85)
In God's love and mercy,
we are given each new day
for the healing of the world.
In the name of Christ, you are forgiven.
In the name of Christ, you are forgiven.

Response to the Word (Isaiah 40, Psalm 85,
2 Peter 3, Mark 1)
God of patience and peace,
as John the Baptizer called the people
to repentance,
so you call us to new life
in your Spirit.
Help us wait for your promised coming,
and prepare your way
with faithfulness and steadfast love. Amen.

THANKSGIVING AND COMMUNION

Offering Prayer (Isaiah 40, Mark 1)
Merciful One,
prepare our hearts to receive anew
the coming of your Son
with fire and the Spirit.
We offer you our thanks and these gifts,
that all may know the power of your love
to transform the world
with justice and righteousness.
(B. J. Beu)

Communion Prayer

God of justice and bounty,
in your new day,
the world is filled with good things.
Bless these gifts of bread and wine,
fruit of the vine and work of human hands,
that they may nourish us as we await your coming,
in the name of Christ, who lived and died
so that we might live. Amen.

Great Thanksgiving

Christ be with you.
And also with you.
Lift up your hearts.
We lift them up to God.
Let us give our thanks to the Holy One.
It is right to give our thanks and praise.

It is a right, good, and a joyful thing,
always and everywhere, to give you thanks.
You lead us in paths of righteousness and peace.
In the words of the prophet Isaiah,
and the cry of John the Baptizer,
you have spoken of your great love
for your people and have promised
to heal all that is broken and forsaken,
to redeem all who are lost and alone.

And so, with your people on earth,
and all the great cloud of witnesses in heaven,
we praise your name and join their unending hymn:
Holy, holy, holy One, God of power and might,
heaven and earth are full of your glory.
Hosanna in the highest.
Blessed is the one who comes
in your holy name.
Hosanna in the highest.

Holy are you, and holy is your child, Jesus Christ,
who came to the river to be baptized,
and taught us of the Holy Spirit,
living in us and around us and among us.

On the night in which he gave himself up
(continue the Words of Institution)
do this in remembrance of me.

And so, in remembrance of your mighty acts
in Jesus Christ, we offer ourselves
in praise and thanksgiving
as a holy and living sacrifice
as we proclaim the mystery of faith.
Christ has died.
Christ is risen.
Christ will come again.

Pour out your Holy Spirit on us gathered here,
and on these gifts of bread and wine.
Make them be for us the body and blood of Christ,
that we may become one with Christ,
who lived and died and rose to bring healing
to a broken world.
By your Spirit make us one with Christ,
one with each other, and one in ministry
to all the world, until we feast together
at the heavenly banquet in your eternal realm.

Maker of justice and mercy,
Spirit of compassion and grace,
Lover of all creation,
we give you thanks and praise.
Amen.

SENDING FORTH

Benediction (Isaiah 40, Mark 1)
Go out to a world that hungers for righteousness.
Prepare the highway for our God:
make ready the paths of peace.
Amen.

CONTEMPORARY OPTIONS

Gathering Words (Isaiah 40, Mark 1)
Prepare the way of the Holy One.
Prepare the way of our God.
Make ready the paths of peace.
Prepare the way of our God.
Make ready your hearts for the coming of the Lord.
Prepare the way of our God.

—*Or*—

Gathering Words (Isaiah 40, Mark 1)
Prepare the way of the Holy One.
Prepare the way of our God.

Praise Sentences
The Holy One gives what is good.
We give our thanks and praise.

DECEMBER 11, 2011

Third Sunday of Advent
Mary J. Scifres

COLOR

Purple

SCRIPTURE READINGS

Isaiah 61:1-4, 8-11; Psalm 126; 1 Thessalonians 5:16-24;
John 1:6-8, 19-28

THEME IDEAS

God's anointed one brings the hope and joy heralded by the
prophets. The birth of Jesus is truly a gift to celebrate. For
with Christ comes hope for the despairing. With Christ
comes the promise of justice and righteousness that brings
freedom to the captives and good news to the oppressed.
We are called to live this dream with goodness in our
thoughts and in our actions. We are called to not only rejoice in this hope but also to pray constantly for this promised reality. The birth of Jesus is truly a gift to celebrate, even
as we face the call to live as people of the dream—people
who dream and work to bring Christ's promise to fruition.

INVITATION AND GATHERING

Call to Worship (Psalm 126, 1 Thessalonians 5)
Come home with shouts of joy,
for Christ's birth is ever near!

**We are like people living a dream,
the dream of Christmas day.**
Carry the promises of God,
for Christ's birth brings new hope.
**Our mouths are filled with laughter,
as we rejoice in this glorious news.**
Come home with thankful hearts,
for Christ's presence is all around.
**We rejoice in glorious hope,
for love has called us here!**

Opening Prayer (Isaiah 61, Psalm 126)
God of justice and love,
 we enter into your presence
 with hopeful hearts.
Gather us in as a well-tended harvest.
Fill our hearts with joy at your promised coming.
Pour out your Spirit upon us,
 that we may be people who dream of justice,
 people who live in righteousness.
Flow through our hearts and our lives,
 that good news and hope may break forth
 into all the world. Amen.

PROCLAMATION AND RESPONSE

Prayer of Confession (Isaiah 61, Psalm 126)
Light of life,
 shine into the darkest places of our lives,
 that we may confess our sins
 and move into the light of your love.
Flow through us,
 that your Spirit may rule our hearts
 and transform our actions
 into justice and righteousness.
Forgive us when we cause weeping and sorrow,
 rather than joy and hope.
Transform us to be people of your dream,

children of Christ's promise,
  and disciples of hope
    for all the world to see. Amen.

Words of Assurance (Psalm 126)

When God restored our fortunes
  through Christ's glorious love,
  we were like those who dream.
We are those who dream!
May our mouths be filled with laughter
  and our tongues with shouts of joy
  as we rejoice in this promise:
    through Christ, we are all forgiven
    and restored to God's holy love.
Amen and amen.

Passing the Peace of Christ (Psalm 126)

Shout for joy! Live in laughter! Share signs of peace and
love with everyone you meet.

Response to the Word (Isaiah 61, Psalm 126)

The Spirit of the Lord God is upon us.
  **Christ sends us to bring good news
  to the oppressed.**
The Spirit of the everlasting God is upon us.
  Christ calls us to bind up the brokenhearted.
The Spirit of God's holy love is upon us.
  Christ cries out for us to release the captives.
The Spirit of Christ Jesus is with us.
  Christ moves us forward into glorious hope.

—Or—

Response to the Word (Isaiah 61, 1 Thessalonians 5)

Make straight the way of the Lord.
  We pray with constant hope.
Bring good news to the oppressed.
  We pray with constant hope.
Care for the brokenhearted.
  We pray with constant hope.

Love justice and live for mercy.
We pray with constant hope.
Make straight the way of our God.
We pray with constant hope.

THANKSGIVING AND COMMUNION

Invitation to the Offering (Psalm 126)
Come home with shouts of joy. Bring forth the sheaves of
God's harvest. As we reflect on the many ways God
blesses us with abundance and joy, let us share those gifts
with others in need.

Offering Prayer (1 Thessalonians 5)
Rejoice always. Pray without ceasing.
Give thanks in all circumstances.
Let us give thanks silently for the myriad ways
    God has blessed us and enabled us
    to be a blessing to others.
(A time of silent prayer follows.)
In praise and hope, we thank you, O God. Amen.

The Great Thanksgiving (Isaiah 61)
The Lord be with you.
And also with you.
Lift up your hearts.
We lift them up to the Lord.
Let us give thanks to the Lord, our God.
It is right to give our thanks and praise.

It is right, and a good and joyful thing,
    always and everywhere to give you thanks,
    Almighty God, creator of heaven and earth.
You formed us in your image,
    and breathed into us the breath of life.
You spoke to us through your prophets,
    revealing your love through challenges
    and promises of hope and justice.
When we turned away and our love failed,

your love remained steadfast.
You delivered us from death and despair
and made an everlasting covenant with us
to endure throughout all the ages.

And so, with your people on earth,
and all the company of heaven,
we praise your name
and join their unending hymn, saying:
Holy, holy, holy Lord, God of power and might,
heaven and earth are full of your glory.
Hosanna in the highest! Blessed is the One
who comes in the name of the Lord.
Hosanna in the highest!

Holy are you, and blessed is your Son, Jesus Christ.
Your Spirit anointed him
to bring good news to the oppressed,
to bind up the brokenhearted,
and to set the captives free.
Even when facing death, Jesus reached out—
to the grieving and sorrowful,
to his mother and his beloved disciple,
even to his betrayer and his denier.
And in that death, you called Christ forth to new life.
You gave birth to your church,
delivered us from the oppression of sin and death,
and made with us a new, everlasting covenant
by water and the Spirit.

With joy and gratitude, we break this bread
and remember the covenant
that welcomes us to this table.
In remembrance of you,
we eat of this bread, even as we remember
those who are hungry this day.
With awe and wonder, we fill this cup
and remember the many ways

that Jesus pours his Spirit into our lives.
In remembrance of you and your abundant love,
> we will drink from this cup, even as we remember
> those who thirst for love and justice.

And so, in remembrance of these,
> your miraculous acts in Christ Jesus,
> we offer ourselves in praise and thanksgiving
> as children of your promise,
> living and dreaming your hope,
> and proclaiming the mystery of our faith.
> **Christ has died.**
> **Christ is risen.**
> **Christ will come again.**

Communion Prayer (Isaiah 61)

Pour out your Holy Spirit on us,
> that we might be sealed
> > in your everlasting covenant.

Pour out your Holy Spirit
> on these gifts of bread and wine,
> > that they might be vessels of help and hope.

Live in us,
> that by your Spirit,
> > we might be one with Christ,
> > one with each other,
> > and one in ministry to all the world,
> > > until Christ comes in final victory
> > > > and we feast at your heavenly banquet.

Through Jesus Christ,
> and with the Holy Spirit in your holy Church,
> > all honor and glory is yours, almighty God,
> > > now and forevermore. Amen.

Giving the Bread and Cup

(The bread and wine are given to the people, with these or other words of blessing.)
The life of Christ, revealed in you.
The love of Christ, flowing through you.

SENDING FORTH

Benediction (Isaiah 61, 1 Thessalonians 5)
Holding fast to what is good,
let us go forth as children of God's promise.
Abstaining from evil,
let us go forth as people of justice
and righteousness.
As faithful followers of Christ,
let us go forth in hope and joy.

CONTEMPORARY OPTIONS

Gathering Words
The Spirit of God is calling.
We come here with shouts of joy!
The voice of Christ is calling.
We come here with shouts of joy!
But listen—for the oppressed are crying out,
the imprisoned are shaking their bars,
the downtrodden are weeping for hope.
How then shall we come with shouts of joy?
We come here to live the dream.
The Spirit gives dreams of justice.
We come here to live the dream.
God calls us to live in righteousness.
We come here to live the dream.
Christ leads us to bring hope to the world.
We come here to live the dream.
As we listen and respond, may we be
like those promised dreamers and visionaries
who make straight God's ways in this world
and who bring the hope of Christ's justice for all.

Praise Sentences (Psalm 126, 1 Thessalonians 5)
God has done great things for us!
Give thanks and praise!
Christ is doing great things for us!
Give thanks and praise!

DECEMBER 18, 2011

Fourth Sunday of Advent
Sandra Miller

COLOR
Purple

SCRIPTURE READINGS
2 Samuel 7:1-11, 16; Luke 1:47-55; Romans 16:25-27;
Luke 1:26-38

THEME IDEAS
The Holy One cannot be confined, not even in a beautiful
house of sweet-smelling cedar. Rather, God is eternal,
planted in us through the ages. It begins with God's promise to Abraham and is reflected in Nathan's words to
David, "Go, do all that you have in mind; for [God] is with
you." God is surely with Elizabeth, and God is with Mary,
the favored one in whom the Holy One is made manifest.
In our faith and in our waiting, Christ is planted in us and
in our global society for the generations to come. Nothing
is impossible with God.

INVITATION AND GATHERING

**Call to Worship (2 Samuel 7, Luke 1:47-55,
Luke 1:26-38)**
Host of Hosts, from sunrise to sunrise,
and generation to generation, we are your people.

You have been with us wherever we have gone.
You will be with us wherever we may go.
You planted us in a land flowing with milk and honey,
then you planted our salvation in Mary's womb.
Jesus, who is the Christ, is planted firmly
in each one of us.
Our souls magnify the Holy One.
Our spirits rejoice in God, our Savior.

Opening Prayer (2 Samuel 7, Luke 1:26-38)
Beloved, Holy Lover,
we welcome you to our house,
the sacred space we have built
to gather together as your people.
Here we come to offer you
our thanksgiving and praise
in response to the abundance
of your creation.
Here we come to share with you
our prayers of confession and petition,
for they lie heavy on our hearts.
Even knowing that you are here
and everywhere,
we come longing to hear you say,
"I am with you always." Amen.

PROCLAMATION AND RESPONSE

Prayer of Confession (Luke 1:47-55)
Compassionate, Forgiving God,
we trespass on your mercy
and take your favor for granted.
We think only of ourselves.
We forget the lessons
of those who came before us,
and ignore our responsibility
to those who will follow us.
We grow proud and seek power.

We do not see the destruction of our actions
and how it distances us from you.
**We do not recognize our hunger for what it is,
or where it leads us.**
We grow faint.
Bring us home to you, Merciful Beloved.

Words of Assurance (Luke 1:47-55)

The Holy One forgives and bestows favor
on each of us, even and especially
when we are lowly in spirit.
We are blessed from generation to generation
by the Mighty One, whose strength and mercy
are forever.

Passing the Peace of Christ

The light and hope of Christ lives in each of us.
The peace of Christ be with you always.
And also with you.

Response to the Word (2 Samuel 7, Luke 1:26-38)

Beloved, when we were in exile,
you dwelled with us in our tents.
When we were afflicted,
you comforted us in your mercy.
Like sheep in the pastures,
you gathered us to you.
In this pregnant time of waiting,
we yearn for the coming of your Son again,
as if for the first time.
For with you, Holy One,
all things are possible.

THANKSGIVING AND COMMUNION

Invitation to the Offering (Luke 1:26-38)

The God of Abundance lays the bounty of all creation before us, strengthens us when we are weak, and fills us when we are hungry. Let us share deeply and joyfully, that all may come to the table of God's heavenly feast.

Offering Prayer (Romans 16:25-27)
God only Wise,
accept these offerings,
the fruit of our labor and lives,
in obedience of our faith,
through Jesus Christ,
to whom be the glory forever!
Amen.

SENDING FORTH

Benediction (Luke 1:47-55, Romans 16, Luke 1:26-38)
Be strengthened according to the proclamation
of Jesus Christ.
Go, do all that you have in mind,
for the Holy One is with you.
Nothing is impossible with God.

CONTEMPORARY OPTIONS

Gathering Words (Luke 1:47-55, Luke 1:26-38)
In the never-ending flow from Abraham to Christ,
in the ever-reaching flow from Christ to the present,
you are planted in Life by the power
of the Holy Mystery, the power of the Holy Spirit.
We are your people; you are our salvation.
Waiting for your coming, rejoicing in your being,
we offer you our hearts, prayers, and praise.
Merciful One, in you we have found our place.

Praise Sentences (Romans 16:25-27)
Glory to God, through Jesus Christ!
Glory forever and ever!
Glory to God whose wisdom knows no bounds.
Glory forever and ever! Amen.

DECEMBER 24, 2011

Christmas Eve

B. J. Beu

COLOR

White

SCRIPTURE READINGS

Isaiah 9:2-7; Psalm 96; Titus 2:11-14; Luke 2:1-20

THEME IDEAS

This is a night for rejoicing—a night to sing a new song to God, a night to celebrate the salvation brought through the birth of Jesus, a night to embrace the light shining in the darkness. God's light and salvation have been brought forth through a child who will rule with justice and righteousness.

INVITATION AND GATHERING

Call to Worship (Isaiah 9, Psalm 96)
We who have walked in darkness
have seen a great light.
    Even in a land of deep darkness—
    on us light has shined.
For a child has been born for us.
God's own Son has been given to us.
    We call him Wonderful Counselor,
    Mighty God, Everlasting Father,

Prince of Peace.
His authority shall grow continually,
and there shall be endless peace
through his glorious reign.
Let all God's people sing for joy.
Let heaven and nature sing!
(This leads naturally into the hymn "Joy to the World.")

Opening Prayer (Isaiah 9, Luke 2)
Shine your light, O God,
into the darkness of our world.
Shine your glory, Holy One,
into the shadows of our lives.
May the singing of the angelic chorus
stir our hearts this night,
as it did the shepherds
as they watched over their flocks by night.
Prepare our hearts anew, O God,
to behold the gift of your Son
in awe and wonder.

PROCLAMATION AND RESPONSE

Call to Prayer (Psalm 96, Isaiah 9)
Let the heavens be glad.
Let the earth rejoice.
Christ judges the people with equity.
Let the people shed tears of joy.
Let the faithful offer shouts of thanksgiving.
Christ judges the world with righteousness
and the peoples with truth.
Let us offer our prayers to the child who leads us—
our Wonderful Counselor and Prince of Peace.

Christmas Eve Litany (Luke 2)
In the midst of a silent night sky, a star beckons:
Rise up, shepherd, and follow.
In the midst of a tranquil field, an angel proclaims:
Rise up, shepherd, and follow.

In the midst of our loneliness and pain, God calls:
Rise up, children, and follow.
With the promise of new life, Christ whispers:
Rise up, children, and follow.

Response to the Word (Luke 2)

There was no room at the inn for Mary and Joseph.
Is there room in our hearts for God's salvation?
May there be room, O God.
May there be room.
There was amazement in the fields at the angel's news.
Is there amazement in our hearts for God's salvation?
May there be amazement, O God.
May there be amazement.
There was joy in Mary's heart as she beheld her son.
Is there joy in our hearts for God's salvation?
May there be joy, O God.
May there be joy.

THANKSGIVING AND COMMUNION

Offering Prayer (1 Corinthians 1)

God of light, author of salvation,
you have given us a gift beyond price—
the gift of your own child,
the gift of everlasting life.
We join the angels and shepherds this night
to celebrate our great joy
as we offer you our gifts—
gifts of our deepest love
and thankfulness.

SENDING FORTH

Benediction (Isaiah 9)

Walk in darkness no longer.
We will walk in the light of Christ.
Treasure the gift of a child who will lead us.
We will treasure the gift of salvation.

Bask in the music of the angelic chorus.
We will bask in the glory of God's love.

CONTEMPORARY OPTIONS

Gathering Words (Isaiah 9)

Jesus is born this very night.
Love is born this very hour.
Light shines in our deepest darkness.
Jesus is born this very night.
Love is born this very hour.

Praise Sentences (Isaiah 9, Luke 2)

God's salvation has come.
Christ is born. Alleluia!
Light has shined in our darkness.
Christ is born. Alleluia!
God's salvation has come.
Alleluia!

DECEMBER 25, 2011

Christmas Day
B. J. Beu

COLOR

White

SCRIPTURE READINGS

Isaiah 52:7-10; Psalm 98; Hebrews 1:1-4, (5-12); John 1:1-14

THEME IDEAS

Although the birth of Jesus is the focus of Christmas, themes of grace and salvation flow from this event and shape today's scripture message. Our need to sing and rejoice as we respond to God's gift of salvation carries throughout the Christmas season. This need is as ancient as the word of God itself. Allow the words and images of today's scriptures to inspire your services of worship, that everyone may glimpse the glory of this ancient miracle and feel its continuing power to transform our lives.

INVITATION AND GATHERING

Call to Worship (John 1, Psalm 98)
In the beginning was the Word,
and the Word was with God,
and the Word was God.
> Make a joyful noise to the Lord, all the earth.
> Let the seas roar and the mountains quake.

Christ was in the beginning with God.
All things came into being through him.
Sing to the Lord a new song,
for God has done marvelous things.
What has come into being in him was life,
and that life was the light of all people.
Let heaven and earth break forth
into joyous song, singing praises to our God.
The light shines in the darkness
and the darkness did not overcome it.
Christ, our light, shines forth in glory.
Christ, our life, brings us grace and truth.
Alleluia!

Opening Prayer (John 1)

God of life and light,
    as you came on that Christmas morning
        so many years ago,
        come to us today.
Gather us into your light and love
    and fill us with the brightness of your glory.
Shine the light of your love
    into the recesses of our lives,
        that we may walk in darkness no longer.
Amen.

PROCLAMATION AND RESPONSE

Prayer of Confession and Assurance (Hebrews 1)

God of love and light,
    you have blessed us with a priceless gift—
        the gift of your very self
          in the person of Jesus.
Forgive us, Holy One,
    when we deny your gift
        or neglect your promise in our lives.
Forgive us, Mighty God,
    when we fail to acknowledge Christ
        as the reflection of your glory and majesty.

Purify our hearts,
purge our sins,
and make us your beloved children,
that we may be full of your righteousness,
grace, and love. Amen.

Words of Assurance (Psalm 98, Hebrews 1)
Christ judges us with righteousness and equity,
and loves us with grace and mercy.
Through the gracious gift of God,
and the gift of Christ, we are forgiven!

THANKSGIVING AND COMMUNION

Offering Prayer
God of infinite chances,
there is no length you will not go to
to offer us the possibility of new life
and the opportunity for redemption.
As we gather in gratitude for the gift of your Son,
receive our thanks and humble appreciation
for all that we receive,
which makes us what we are.
Bless these gifts and offerings,
that they may bring light and life
to God's people. Amen.

SENDING FORTH

Benediction (Isaiah 52, John 1)
Walk in darkness no longer.
We will walk in the light of Christ.
Sing of salvation and peace.
We will live with grace and joy.
Go and proclaim the good news,
Jesus Christ is born. Alleluia!

CONTEMPORARY OPTIONS

Gathering Words (Isaiah 52, Psalm 98)
Sing to the Lord a new song.
We sing of light in our darkness.
Sing to the Lord a new song.
We rejoice in our salvation.
Sing to the Lord a new song.
The Lord is here, alleluia!
Sing to the Lord.

Praise Sentences (Psalm 98)
Glory to God in the highest!
Sing to the Lord a new song!
Christ is born!
Sing to the Lord a new song!
Glory to God in the highest!
Sing to the Lord a new song!

DECEMBER 31, 2011

Watch Night / New Year
Linda Hess

COLOR
White

SCRIPTURE READINGS
Ecclesiastes 3:1-13; Psalm 8; Matthew 25:31-46;
Revelation 21:1-6a

THEME IDEAS
God is the giver of all that we experience. Whether we
view these experiences as positive or negative is largely
up to us and affects our approach to life. Looking to God
in all of life's circumstances is vital to experiencing the gift
of eternal life promised through Christ. Our interconnect-
edness with one another is essential to our connection to
God, and the way we respond to the needs of others is a
visible demonstration of our relationship with God.

INVITATION AND GATHERING

*Call to Worship (Psalm 8, Ecclesiastes 3,
Revelation 21)*
O Lord, our Lord, how majestic is your name
in all the earth!
You have set your glory above the heavens.

From the lips of children and infants,
you ordain praise and thanksgiving
to silence the foe and the avenger.
  You make everything beautiful
  in its own time.
You set eternity in our hearts,
yet we cannot fathom what you have done
from beginning to end.
  What could be better than to be happy
  and to do good while we live?
O Lord, our Lord, how majestic is your name
in all the earth!
  O God, our God, you are Alpha and Omega,
  the Beginning and the End.

Opening Prayer (Revelation 21, Matthew 25)
We come to you today (*tonight*), God,
  the Alpha and the Omega,
    as people blessed by your tender care.
Today (*Tonight*), we come to seek your guidance,
  that we may better understand how to follow
    the teaching of Christ, our Lord and Savior,
      in whose name we pray. Amen.

PROCLAMATION AND RESPONSE

Prayer of Confession (Ecclesiastes 3)
Gracious God, giver of new beginnings,
we come to you today (*tonight*), confessing our need.
  As we face this coming year,
  help us through each day.
As we leave the past year behind,
help us look to you.
  When we face birth or death;
  when we confront a time to plant or to uproot,
  help us put our faith in you.
When we see a time to tear down or to build up,
when we face a time to weep or to laugh,

when we meet a time to be silent or a time to speak,
help us rely on you.
  You alone know what the coming year holds.
  You alone know of our small triumphs
  and our grand failures.
Gracious God, assure us once again
that there is forgiveness in your love.
  Heal us with the knowledge
  that our sins may be left with you,
  through our Savior, Jesus Christ. Amen.

Words of Assurance (Ecclesiastes 3, Matthew 25)

God brings a season for every activity under heaven
  and has made everything beautiful in its time.
Although we cannot fathom the depths of God's love,
  we know that God cares for each of us;
  we know that our inheritance comes from God.

Passing the Peace of Christ (Philippians 4)

May the peace of God, which passes all understanding,
be with you. Share this gift of peace with all whom you
see and greet.

Response to the Word (Matthew 25, Psalm 8, Ecclesiastes 3)

Let all you who are blessed by God come and take your
inheritance, and in your hearts receive the gift of eternal
life promised by God. Celebrate the majesty of God's
name in all the earth!

THANKSGIVING AND COMMUNION

Invitation to the Offering (Matthew 25)

We are here to give our gifts, as Jesus has taught us. To
those who are hungry and thirsty, let us offer food and
drink that they may be satisfied. To those in need of clothing, let us offer to clothe them. To those who are sick, let
us offer them our care. To those in prison, let us offer the
gift of our presence as we visit them. We remember, as

Jesus has told us, that whatever we do for the least of our brothers and sisters, we do for Christ. May the gifts we give today (*tonight*) be a demonstration of our love for God, and may they maintain and expand the work of this congregation.

Offering Prayer (Matthew 25)

God, source of all we have,
    help us remember the tasks
        that you have set before us.
Bless these gifts,
    that they may help continue
        the work we are called to do.
Use this place and this congregation
    to reflect the love that Christ has shown us. Amen.

SENDING FORTH

Benediction (Ecclesiastes 3)

Go forth with happiness and with good works.
    This is what God has called us to do.
Find satisfaction in all your toil.
    This is the gift of God.
In everything you do, praise the Lord!
    Amen.

CONTEMPORARY OPTIONS

Gathering Words (Matthew 25)

All who hunger and thirst are welcome here.
    Come find the food and drink
    that does not perish.
All who are strangers are welcome here.
    When it's time to leave,
    we'll part as friends.
All who don't know where to turn are welcome here.
    Come and find the living God,
    who helps us find our way.
Thanks be to God.

Praise Sentences (Psalm 8)
God, you are an awesome and a mighty God!
We see your glory in the heavens above
and in the earth below!
We see the work of your hands when we behold
the moon and the stars.
We see you in everything that is.
We see the work of your fingers
when we look at the flocks and herds,
the beasts of the field, the birds of the air,
and the fish of the sea.
We praise your name continually
and marvel at your creation!
God, you are an awesome and a mighty God!
We see your glory in the heavens above
and in the earth below!

CONTRIBUTORS

Peter Bankson
Peter Bankson is a Steward and part of the Servant Leadership Team of Seekers Church, a Church of the Saviour congregation in Washington, DC.

Laura Jaquith Bartlett
Laura Jaquith Bartlett, an ordained minister of music and worship, lives at a United Methodist retreat center in the foothills of Oregon's Mt. Hood.

B. J. Beu
B. J. Beu is senior pastor of Neighborhood Congregational Church in Laguna Beach, California. A graduate of Boston University and Pacific Lutheran University, Beu loves creative worship, preaching, and advocating for peace and justice.

Mary Petrina Boyd
Mary Petrina Boyd is pastor of Seattle First United Methodist Church. She spends alternate summers working as an archaeologist in Jordan.

Joanne Carlson Brown
Joanne Carlson Brown is the clergy-type for Tibbetts United Methodist Church in Seattle, WA. She is also an adjunct professor at Seattle University School of Theology and Ministry and lives in Seattle with Thistle, the wee Westie.

Ken Burton
Ken Burton is a member of the Celebration Circle Mission Group of Seekers Church in Washington, DC.

Shelley Cunningham
Shelley Cunningham is a pastor at Christ the King Lutheran Church (ELCA) in New Brighton, Minnesota. She also writes for Luther Seminary's alumni magazine, *The Story,* and its online daily devotional, *God Pause.*

Roberta J. Egli
Roberta J. Egli serves as pastor to Englewood United Methodist Church in Salem, Oregon, and is the director of Deep Well Ministry in Corvallis, where she offers spiritual direction for individuals and small groups, facilitates spiritual formation retreats, and serves as a worship resource consultant.

Rebecca J. Kruger Gaudino
Rebecca J. Kruger Gaudino, a United Church of Christ minister in Portland, Oregon, teaches world religions and biblical studies as Visiting Professor at the University of Portland and also writes for the Church.

Jamie D. Greening
Jamie D. Greening has served as the senior pastor of First Baptist Church in Port Orchard, Washington, for ten years.

Linda Hess
Linda Hess lives near the shore in Delaware, where she writes Christian songs and other inspirational pieces.

Hans Holznagel
Hans Holznagel has served for more than twenty-five years on the national staff of the United Church of Christ as a journalist, communication officer, mission interpreter, administrator, and fundraiser. He belongs to Archwood United Church of Christ in Cleveland, Ohio.

Bill Hoppe
Bill Hoppe is the music coordinator for Bear Creek United Methodist Church in Woodinville, Washington, and is a

member of the band BrokenWorks, for which he is the keyboardist. He thanks his family and friends for their continued love, support, and inspiration.

Beryl Ingram

Beryl Ingram is an Elder in the United Methodist Church, and senior pastor of First United Methodist Church in Bellevue, Washington. She is delirious with joy at the turn-around taking place in that congregation, and is especially thankful for the young families and babies who provide an endless witness to God's creative energies!

Sara Dunning Lambert

Sara Dunning Lambert is mom, wife, nurse, child of God, and Worship Coordinator at Bear Creek United Methodist Church in Woodinville, Washington.

Marcia McFee

Marcia McFee, Ph.D., is a consultant on worship and produces an online planning resource, *The Worship Design Studio*.

Sandra Miller

Sandra Miller is a member of Celebration Circle, the worship leader and liturgy team of Seekers Church, a lay-led ecumenical church in the tradition of Church of the Saviour in Washington, DC. Sandra has a deep love of religious ritual developed as a child raised in the Orthodox Jewish faith. Christ called Sandra nearly twelve years ago.

Matthew J. Packer

Matthew J. Packer is a music director at Flushing United Methodist Church in Flushing, Michigan, and an M.Div. student at Methodist Theological School in Delaware, Ohio.

Bryan Schneider-Thomas

Bryan Schneider-Thomas is the pastor of Amble United Methodist Church near Howard City, Michigan, and serves churches as a consultant in art and architecture.

Mary J. Scifres

Mary J. Scifres serves as a consultant in leadership, church and culture, worship, and evangelism from her Laguna Beach home, where she and her spouse B. J. reside with their teenage son, Michael. Her books include *The United Methodist Music and Worship Planner, Prepare!* and *Searching for Seekers.*

Deborah Sokolove

Deborah Sokolove is the director of the Henry Luce III Center for the Arts and Religion at Wesley Theological Seminary, and writes liturgy for Seekers Church, an ecumenical Christian community in Washington, DC.

Leigh Anne Taylor

Leigh Anne Taylor lives, writes, and makes music with her family in the beautiful Blue Ridge Mountains of Virginia.

SCRIPTURE INDEX

(Page numbers in italic refer to pages found only on the CD-ROM)

COMMUNION LITURGIES INDEX

In order of appearance

SONG AND HYMN INDEX

FOOTWASHING PRAYERS AND LITURGIES INDEX

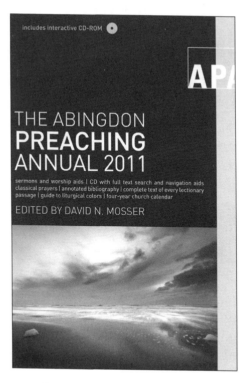

Preachers have long turned to *The Abingdon Preaching Annual* for help with the central task of their ministry: sermon preparation. The 2011 edition of the *Annual* continues this fine tradition with lectionary-based and topical sermons for flexibility in choice, additional lectionary commentary, and worship aids for every sermon. The CD-ROM, included with every book, provides classical and contemporary affirmations and prayers, plus hyperlinked planning aids such as bibliographical references, and the full lectionary texts for each Sunday. *The Abingdon Preaching Annual* is now one of the most comprehensive and useful resources for sermon preparation that you will find on the market.

"Commendations to Abingdon Press for offering two fresh ecumenical resources for pastors."

For *The Abingdon Preaching Annual*—"Anyone who dares proclaim a holy word week in and week out soon realizes that creative inspiration for toe-shaking sermons quickly wanes. Multitasking pastors who are wise seek out resources that multiply their own inductive initiatives."

For *The Abingdon Worship Annual*—"Not only the sermon but also the whole service dares to be toe-shaking . . . and the *Worship Annual* is a reservoir of resources in that direction."

—The Reverend Willard E. Roth, Academy of Parish Clergy President, *Sharing the Practice: The Journal of the Academy of Parish Clergy*

Do you have the book you need?

We want you to have the best planner, designed to meet your specific needs. How do you know if you have the right resource? Simply complete this one-question quiz:

Do you lead worship in a United Methodist congregation?

Yes.

Use *The United Methodist Music and Worship Planner, 2010–2011*
(ISBN: 9781426706486)

No.

Use *Prepare! A Weekly Worship Planbook for Pastors and Musicians, 2010–2011*
(ISBN: 9781426706479)

To order these resources, call Cokesbury Music Service toll-free at 1-877-877-8674, visit your local Cokesbury store, or shop online at www.cokesbury.com. Do you find yourself rushing at the last minute to order your new planner? Subscribe today and receive your new *The United Methodist Music and Worship Planner* or *Prepare!* automatically next year and every year. Call toll-free 1-800-672-1789 to request subscription.

Abingdon Press